**New Directions for
Institutional Research**

J. Fredericks Volkwein
EDITOR-IN-CHIEF

Robert K. Toutkoushian
ASSOCIATE EDITOR

D1527613

Successful
Strategic
Planning

Michael J. Dooris
John M. Kelley
James F. Trainer
EDITORS

Number 123 • Fall 2004
Jossey-Bass
San Francisco

SUCCESSFUL STRATEGIC PLANNING
Michael J. Dooris, John M. Kelley, James F. Trainer (eds.)
New Directions for Institutional Research, no. 123
J. Fredericks Volkwein, Editor-in-Chief

Copyright © 2004 Wiley Periodicals, Inc., A Wiley Company

All rights reserved. No part of this publication may be reproduced in any form or by any means, except as permitted under sections 107 or 108 of the 1976 United States Copyright Act, without either the prior written permission of the publisher or authorization through the Copyright Clearance Center, 222 Rosewood Drive, Danvers, MA 01923; (978) 750-8400; fax (978) 646-8600. The code and copyright notice appearing at the bottom of the first page of an article in this journal indicate the copyright holder's consent that copies may be made for personal or internal use, or for personal or internal use of specific clients, on the condition that the copier pay for copying beyond that permitted by law. This consent does not extend to other kinds of copying, such as copying for general distribution, for advertising or promotional purposes, for creating collective works, or for resale. Such permission requests and other permission inquiries should be addressed to the Permissions Department, c/o John Wiley & Sons, Inc., 111 River St., Hoboken, NJ 07030; (201) 748-8789, fax (201) 748-6326, http://www.wiley.com/go/permissions.

NEW DIRECTIONS FOR INSTITUTIONAL RESEARCH (ISSN 0271-0579, electronic ISSN 1536-075X) is part of The Jossey-Bass Higher and Adult Education Series and is published quarterly by Wiley Subscription Services, Inc., A Wiley Company, at Jossey-Bass, 989 Market Street, San Francisco, California 94103-1741 (publication number USPS 098-830). Periodicals Postage Paid at San Francisco, California, and at additional mailing offices. POSTMASTER: Send address changes to New Directions for Institutional Research, Jossey-Bass, 989 Market Street, San Francisco, California 94103-1741.

SUBSCRIPTIONS cost $80.00 for individuals and $150.00 for institutions, agencies, and libraries. See order form at end of book.

EDITORIAL CORRESPONDENCE should be sent to J. Fredericks Volkwein, Center for the Study of Higher Education, Penn State University, 400 Rackley Building, University Park, PA 16801-5252.

New Directions for Institutional Research is indexed in College Student Personnel Abstracts, Contents Pages in Education, and Current Index to Journals in Education (ERIC).

Microfilm copies of issues and chapters are available in 16mm and 35mm, as well as microfiche in 105mm, through University Microfilms Inc., 300 North Zeeb Road, Ann Arbor, Michigan 48106-1346.

ISBN 0-7879-7792-6

www.josseybass.com

THE ASSOCIATION FOR INSTITUTIONAL RESEARCH was created in 1966 to benefit, assist, and advance research leading to improved understanding, planning, and operation of institutions of higher education. Publication policy is set by its Publications Committee.

PUBLICATIONS COMMITTEE

Andreea M. Serban (Chair)	Santa Barbara City College
Trudy H. Bers	Oakton Community College
Stephen L. DesJardins	University of Michigan
Eric L. Dey	University of Michigan
Laura W. Perna	University of Maryland
Stephen R. Porter	Wesleyan University
Jeffrey A. Seybert	Johnson County Community College

EX-OFFICIO MEMBERS OF THE PUBLICATIONS COMMITTEE

Timothy K. C. Chow	Rose-Hulman Institute of Technology
Anne Marie Delaney	Babson College
Richard D. Howard	Montana State University–Bozeman
Gerald W. McLaughlin	DePaul University
John C. Smart	University of Memphis
J. Fredericks Volkwein	Pennsylvania State University

For information about the Association for Institutional Research, write to the following address:

AIR Executive Office
114 Stone Building
Florida State University
Tallahassee, FL 32306-4462

(850) 644-4470

air@mailer.fsu.edu
http://airweb.org

CONTENTS

PART TWO: Examples from the Field

James F. Trainer

This final chapter integrates the entire volume by examining several strategic planning models and their intersection with other institutional research activities. The chapter also offers an annotated list of "top-ten" planning tools, as well as key strategic planning references.

EDITORS' NOTES

Institutional research (IR) has long been expected to bring to colleges or universities a high level of what Patrick Terenzini (1999, p. 23) calls "organizational intelligence," and to serve as what Marvin Petersen terms a "proactive management guide" (1999, p. 103). To the extent that IR provides information and analyses in support of policy formulation, organizational decision making, and improvement, knowledge about strategic planning can be viewed as part of the fundamental, relevant IR skill set.

In the twenty-fifth anniversary issue of *New Directions for Institutional Research*, J. Fredericks Volkwein (1999) classified NDIR volumes from 1974 through 1999 into seven topical areas. Twenty-four of the 103 volumes were in the area of "policy, planning, and governance," and among those, eight specifically concerned "planning and strategic planning." Those eight NDIR titles represented the work of an impressive group of contributors, among them editors Paul Dressel, David Hopkins, Roger Schroeder, Robert Fenske, Richard Heydinger, Melvin Hipps, Norman Uhl, Patrick Callan, Frank Schmidtlein, and Toby Milton.

It has been fourteen years since the most recent of those monographs (by Schmidtlein and Milton in 1990), so we are pleased that the *NDIR* series is revisiting this important topic. As editors, we are humbled by the work of the scholarly practitioners who have preceded us, but we take pleasure in presenting the insights of the contributors contained in this issue.

The introductory chapter of this volume briefly reviews the development and evolution of strategic planning in higher education. In Chapter Two, Ann Dodd follows with an overview of changes in accreditation standards and a summary of three effectiveness and quality assurance models; her chapter suggests that accreditation serves as a catalyst for understanding and enhancing institutional effectiveness. In the third chapter, John Jasinski extends Dodd's discussion of the Malcolm Baldrige National Quality Award by examining eleven lessons learned from Baldrige best-practice organizations. Additional lessons are suggested by Craig Clagett in the fourth chapter. He presents readers with three examples of ad hoc institutional research that had a surprisingly strong influence on effective long-term planning. In the fifth chapter, Daniel Seymour, John Kelley, and John Jasinski explicate the systems thinking and other concepts that link planning, organizational improvement, and IR.

The remaining chapters share real-world, hands-on examples of IR and planning practices at various institutions. Seymour demonstrates how planning, improvement, and IR are linked at Los Angeles City College by means of an effective series of plan-act-check loops. Heather Haberaecker connects strategic planning and budgeting in a chapter that could well be subtitled "What Every Planner and Institutional Researcher Needs to Know about Budgeting." Louise Sandmeyer, Michael Dooris, and Robert Barlock present a case study of how integrated planning connects planning for facilities, enrollments, budgets, and staffing at Penn State. John Kelley and James Trainer describe Villanova's team approach to goal attainment. A chapter by Chester Warzynski describes the "future search" tool and how it has been useful at Cornell University. Clagett presents an overview of Carroll Community College's strategic planning process. Kathleen Paris shows how to help move a strategic plan off the shelf and into action, citing a University of Wisconsin-Madison case study. In the final chapter, Trainer looks at planning models, techniques, and tools that can be particularly effective in helping to advance planning at any level; he closes with an annotated "pick six" of recommended readings.

The chapters reflect our belief that institutional research can and should be a practical, proactive expression of "organizational intelligence," and that linkages among strategic planning, effective IR, and organizational improvement are therefore natural and healthy. We hope that this volume is useful to our colleagues.

Michael J. Dooris
John M. Kelley
James F. Trainer
Editors

References

Petersen, M. W. "The Role of Institutional Research: From Improvement to Redesign." In J. F. Volkwein (ed.), *What Is Institutional Research All About? A Critical and Comprehensive Assessment of the Profession*. New Directions for Institutional Research, no. 104. San Francisco: Jossey-Bass, 1999.

Schmidtlein, F. A., and Milton, T. H. (eds.). *Adapting Strategic Planning to Campus Realities*. New Directions for Institutional Research, no. 67. San Francisco: Jossey-Bass, 1990.

Terenzini, P. T. "On the Nature of Institutional Research and the Knowledge and Skills It Requires." In J. F. Volkwein (ed.), *What Is Institutional Research All About? A Critical and Comprehensive Assessment of the Profession*. New Directions for Institutional Research, no. 104. San Francisco: Jossey-Bass, 1999.

Volkwein, J. F. (ed.). *What Is Institutional Research All About? A Critical and Comprehensive Assessment of the Profession*. New Directions for Institutional Research, no. 104. San Francisco: Jossey-Bass, 1999.

MICHAEL J. DOORIS *is director of planning research and assessment at Penn State University, in the Office of Planning and Institutional Assessment.*

JOHN M. KELLEY *is executive director of the Office of Planning, Training, and Institutional Research at Villanova University.*

JAMES F. TRAINER *is director of planning and assessment at Villanova University.*

PART ONE

The Foundations of Strategic Planning

*The authors present an overview of strategic planning,
examine its history and mystique, and conclude that
planning, if properly implemented, can have a powerful
impact on advancing and transforming colleges and
universities.*

Strategic Planning in Higher Education

Michael J. Dooris, John M. Kelley, James F. Trainer

Homo sapiens is the classical term used by philosophers to elevate humankind from the remainder of creation. The term, of course, refers to our ability to think, conceptualize, mull, peruse, and innovate. It also extends to
other defining functions and faculties, such as problem solving and imagination. Rationality certainly characterizes most jobs and professions, but it
crescendos in the world of strategic planning.

The editors of this volume believe that the soul of strategic planning is
this human capacity for *intentionality*—this ability to formulate goals and
proceed toward them with direct intent.

Planning, Intentionality, and Human Behavior

The Frenchman Henri Fayol, a parent of organizational theory, implicitly
dealt with the notion of "intentionality." In the early 1900s he described
planning as assessing the future, setting goals, and devising ways to bring
about these goals. Mintzberg and Quinn (1996, p. 10) were thinking along
these same lines when, speaking about strategy as plan, they specified two
essential characteristics about strategy: it is made in advance to the actions
to which it applies, and it is developed consciously and purposefully.[1]

Herein, then, lies the essence of strategic planning. When we strip away
the models, schema, and paradigms; when we discard the PowerPoint presentations; and when we look beyond the grids, scorecards and matrices,
we confront our ability to think with intention. Planning concerns an ability that is awakened by the human appetite to better our condition. In the
business world, bettering one's condition includes capturing market share
and improving profits. In higher education, bettering one's condition

includes hiring better faculty, recruiting stronger students, upgrading facilities, strengthening academic programs and student services, and acquiring the resources needed to accomplish these things. Since most institutions of higher education share a similar mission and compete for these same objectives, an essential part of strategic planning involves shaping the institution in ways that ensure mission attainment by capturing and maintaining a market niche in the quest for resources, faculty, and students. Thus strategic planning has both external and internal faces.

Strategic Planning as Formal Practice

Considered in the context of human thought and behavior, planning is certainly not new. To the contrary—since planning embodies essential features of *Homo sapiens,* it is by definition as old as humankind.

On the other hand, when one views strategic planning as a structured management discipline and practice, it is barely out of its infancy. The date on the birth certificate of strategic planning is smudged, but it seems safe to say that it emerged as a distinct methodology sometime between the 1950s and the 1970s. Steiner (1979) asserted that formal strategic planning with its modern design characteristics was first introduced under the rubric of "long-term planning" in the mid-1950s by large companies and conglomerates; Mintzberg (1994a) wrote that it "arrived on the scene" in the mid-1960s when "corporate leaders embraced it as 'the one best way' to devise and implement strategies that would enhance the competitiveness of each business unit." Others attribute the emergence of strategic planning to the turbulent environment of the 1970s when, with the energy crisis and other unanticipated events, organizations scurried to find a more pertinant planning system (Rosenberg and Schewe, 1985).

Many would argue that searching for the birthstone of strategic planning is chimerical since planning is an evolutionary process. Certain dating stones can be located, but strategic planning possesses no single event of origin. What is clear, however, is that the last several decades have been a boom period for strategic planning—a development in which higher education has shared.

Strategic Planning in Higher Education

Higher education's courtship with strategic planning was originally focused on facilities and space planning during an era of rapid expansion. The first significant formal meeting of higher education planners was a 1959 summer program attended by twenty-five campus planners at the Massachusetts Institute of Technology. With sporadic meetings through subsequent years, key members of that group (all with physical planning backgrounds) eventually founded the Society for College and University Planning (SCUP) in 1966 with a base of more than three hundred members, most with a primary interest in campus physical planning (Holmes, 1985).

The environment for higher education began to experience notable unsteadiness in the 1970s with demographic, economic, and technological swerves. Higher education costs began to consistently outpace inflation, and foundational stress fractures were detected in the public's support for higher education. Ideas about planning began to change. The 1983 publication of George Keller's *Academic Strategy* marks a pivot for a shift that occurred around that time, as colleges and universities took a closer look at strategic planning. The 1980s' conception of planning emphasized its use as a rational tool for orderly, systematic advancement of the academic enterprise. Guided by an ennobling mission, institutional leaders could march through a series of prescribed steps and actualize their vision. Linear approaches flourished, featuring a cognitive procession of functions: identifying and prioritizing key stakeholders, environmental scanning, situational analysis such as SWOT, specification of core competencies and distinctive competencies, strategy formulation such as TOWS, goal setting, objective setting, action step setting culminating in alpha-omega activity, and evaluative feedback loops. There is much to be said for these rational models, and they continue to propagate fresh sprouts, notably the Baldrige Educational Criteria for Performance Excellence (for example, Baldrige, 2003) and the Balanced Scorecard (Kaplan and Norton, 1996).

From the 1980s through the end of the century, the visibility and volume of strategic planning in the academy continued to ascend. Keller's 1983 seminal work was named the most influential higher education book of the decade by both the *New York Times* and *Change* magazine. By the 1990s, accreditors were touting strategic planning as a *sine qua non* of organizational effectiveness. The 1998 Council for Higher Education Accreditation's *Recognition Standards* set forth an expectation for "evidence of policies and procedures that stress planning and implementing strategies for change" (CHEA, 1998, p. 7).

By the first year of the new millennium, SCUP membership had swelled to forty-two hundred, and its topical breadth grown to a full range of strategic considerations: governance, budgeting, learning assessment, faculty workload, student engagement, market segmentation, endowment management, and so on.

Three Themes

Three themes, embryonically apparent in the 1990s, have come to maturity. First, a rational-deductive, formulaic approach to strategic planning is being tempered with a cultural-environmental-political perspective. Bryson described this theme vividly: "Most of these new management innovations have tried to improve government decision making and operations by imposing a formal rationality on systems that are not rational, at least in the conventional meaning of the word. Public and nonprofit organizations (and communities) are *politically rational.* . . . The various policies and programs are, in effect, treaties among the various stakeholder groups" (Bryson, 1995, pp. 10–11, emphasis in original).

Second, strategic planning is now increasingly about learning and creativity, with the recognition that college and university leaders need to challenge assumptions and consider radically changing existing structures and processes. Relatively recent conceptions of strategic planning center more on dynamism, flexibility, nimbleness, inventiveness, and imagination. They focus on strategic thinking as opposed to syllogistic analysis. In this vein, Henry Mintzberg observed: "Strategic thinking, in contrast, is about *synthesis*. It involves intuition and creativity" (1994a, p. 108). Bryson eloquently admonished: "Indeed if any particular approach to strategic planning gets in the way of strategic thought and action, that planning approach should be scrapped" (Bryson, 1995, p. 3). Flexibility is a key to organizational success today (Hussey, 1999).

Third, there is a new and powerful emphasis on moving from formulation to implementation, from plan to practice, following Benjamin Franklin's aphorism that "well done is better than well said." More and more administrators are asserting that the purpose of planning is not to make a plan but to make a change. In fact, it is not easy to find a text in today's business schools entitled "Strategic Planning." Most authors prefer the moniker "strategic management," which is meant to embody both thinking and doing. John Bryson speaks of this, in a touching confession in the Preface to the second edition of his acclaimed *Strategic Planning for Public and Nonprofit Organizations:* "The second edition thus reflects a major trend in the field. . . . People also realize that it is not enough just to think— organizations must act as well. And it is not enough just to decide what to do and how to do it—the doing matters too. . . . The result is a book that is as much about strategic management as about strategic planning. I have kept the original title, however, because of the recognition and following the first edition achieved" (1995, p. x).

Critiques of Strategic Planning

Strategic planning is not uniformly applauded. Some have questioned whether it is a vital process, a core function, or the latest fashion in the technique boutique. Williams's canine comparison tugs at our hearts as he laments that strategic planning "lies still and vapid like a tired old fox terrier on the couch. An occasional bark, but no bite" (2000, p. 64).

Upon scrutiny, some of these soothsaying scholars are actually offering a strawman argument in order to criticize strategic planning efforts and trends that go astray, before offering their prescription for success. Robert Birnbaum (2000) focused on higher education's adoption of management "fads," among them strategic planning. Rosenberg and Schewe (1985) contend that strategic plans succeed only 10 percent of the time; they rail against such defects in the planning process as mechanical treatment of the environment, separation of planners from operators, and resistance of organizational cultures. Sevier's recent words are scorching: "There are probably few phrases that cause a greater group groan on most campuses than 'strategic planning.' The fact is, most colleges and universities look at strategic planning as a path to pain, rather than a path to plenty" (2003, p. 18.).

Then Sevier quickly reverses field, logs a number of lessons learned, and concludes that strategic planning "remains a powerful tool for advancing a college's or university's vision" (p. 19).

Harsh as the criticisms appear, they are largely targeted at poor practices that impede creative planning, and the critics, as noted, often offer stories of both failure and success. Mintzberg, perhaps the most cited writer in the field, makes a compelling scholarly argument in his solidly researched 1994 text (Mintzberg, 1994b). He presented considerable evidence that organizations have often had a counterproductive love affair with planning, weighted down by "lead boots" and slowed down by "paperwork mills." Mintzberg also, however, offsets those negative evaluations with a number of corporate success stories spotlighting approaches that were less rational, structured, and rigid. Tom Peters (1994) offered similar ideas (with a lighter touch), hanging the torturous term "death by a thousand initiatives" on strategic planning and other management trends.

So, Does Strategic Planning Work in Higher Education?

Confirmation bias is a well-accepted principle in social science research. As human beings, we are genetically programmed to seek patterns, to conform cognitive input to what we already know, to explain what we see on the basis of our beliefs about how the world works. Especially in the absence of sound empirical analysis, observers—including the editors and authors of this volume—are prone to see the answers we expect to questions such as, "Does strategic planning work?"

After reviewing the literature and consulting with knowledgeable colleagues, we have concluded that a convincing, generalizable empirical study on the efficacy of strategic planning in higher education has yet to be published. There is, of course, no shortage of anecdotes from both sides of the aisle—that is, from the proponents and the critics of strategic planning in academe. Even in the case studies offered by the authors in this volume, there is no definitive answer to the question.

The research design needed to address the effectiveness of strategic planning poses many challenges. Strategic planning in a college or university occurs in a complex, dynamic, real-world environment, not readily amenable to controlled studies, or even to quasi-experimental designs. It is difficult to parse out the measurable effects of strategic planning from the influences of such other important factors as institutional leadership, demographic change, fluctuations in state and federal funding, politics, the actions of competing organizations, social and cultural forces, and the like. Thus, to the best of our knowledge, the present empirical evidence about whether strategic planning does or does not work in higher education is less than conclusive.

Implications

Although we understand and agree that skepticism is warranted from a social science perspective, it is fair to note that on the basis of our research, experiences, and reading of the literature, we are proponents of planning. We find that the central lesson from such critical observers, carefully read, is not that strategic planning does not work; instead, we believe that a more defensible conclusion is that planning can be done poorly or it can be done well. Strategic planning can produce successful results, or it can be ineffective.

We are encouraged by the cases and advice related by the contributors to this volume. We thank our colleagues for sharing their thoughts on how, in the real world in which colleges and universities operate, strategic planning—wisely used—can be a powerful tool to help an academic organization listen to its constituencies, encourage the emergence of good ideas from all levels, recognize opportunities, make decisions supported by evidence, strive toward shared mission. . . . and actualize the vision.

Note

1. Mintzberg and Quinn (1996) also discuss a perspective of strategy "as pattern" that defines strategy as consistency in behavior, whether or not intended. This theme is extended in Mintzberg, Ahlstrand, and Lampel (1998), *Strategy Safari*, a fascinating work that describes and offers the historical foundations of ten distinct schools of thought on strategy formation.

References

Baldrige National Quality Program. *Education Criteria for Performance Excellence.* Gaithersburg, Md.: National Institute of Standards and Technology, U.S. Department of Commerce, 2003.

Birnbaum, R. *Management Fads in Higher Education: Where They Came from, What They Do, Why They Fail.* San Francisco: Jossey-Bass, 2000.

Bryson, J. *Strategic Planning for Public and Nonprofit Organizations* (Rev. ed.). San Francisco: Jossey-Bass, 1995.

Council for Higher Education Accreditation. *1998 Recognition Standards.* CHEA, 1998. http://www.chea.org; retrieved Jan. 2002.

Holmes, J. *20/20 Planning.* Ann Arbor, Mich.: Society for College and University Planning, 1985.

Hussey, D. *Strategy and Planning: A Manager's Guide.* Chichester, England: Wiley, 1999.

Kaplan, R., and Norton, D. *The Balanced Scorecard.* Boston: Harvard Business School Press, 1996.

Keller, G. *Academic Strategy: The Management Revolution in American Higher Education.* Baltimore, Md.: Johns Hopkins University Press, 1983.

Mintzberg, H. "The Fall and Rise of Strategic Planning." *Harvard Business Review*, 1994a, 72(1), 107–114.

Mintzberg, H. *The Rise and Fall of Strategic Planning: Reconceiving Roles for Planning, Plans, Planners.* New York: Free Press, 1994b.

Mintzberg, H., Ahlstrand, B., and Lampel, J. *Strategy Safari: A Guided Tour Through the Wilds of Strategic Management.* New York: Free Press, 1998.

Mintzberg, H., and Quinn, J. B. *Strategy Process* (3rd ed.). Upper Saddle River, N.J.: Prentice Hall, 1996.

Peters, T. *The Pursuit of Wow!* New York: Vintage Books, 1994.

Rosenberg, L. J., and Schewe, C. D. "Strategic Planning: Fulfilling the Promise." *Business Horizons*, 1985, 28(4), 54–62.

Sevier, R. A. "From Strategy to Action." *University Business*, 2003, 6(2), 18–19.

Steiner, G. A. *Strategic Planning: What Every Manager Must Know.* New York: Free Press, 1979.

Williams, R. "Out with the Old, in with the New." *Currents*, 2000, 27(1), 64.

MICHAEL J. DOORIS is director of planning research and assessment at Penn State University, in the Office of Planning and Institutional Assessment.

JOHN M. KELLEY is executive director of the Office of Planning, Training, and Institutional Research at Villanova University.

JAMES F. TRAINER is director of planning and assessment at Villanova University.

2

Accreditation bodies increasingly force institutions to merge their accountability reporting, institutional research, outcomes assessment, and decision-making activities, thus serving as catalysts for enhancing institutional effectiveness.

Accreditation as a Catalyst for Institutional Effectiveness

Ann H. Dodd

Accreditation is a fact of life in higher education; the reaccreditation cycle includes both periodic self-assessment and external review by peers. It is perhaps the most prominent of all accountability efforts. It also happens to be one of the initiatives to which institutional research staff can add significant value. This chapter defines the importance of accreditation to higher education, details the potential role of institutional research in the reaccreditation cycle, and proposes that institutional research can play an important role in an integrated approach to institutional effectiveness where accreditation activities are fully linked to ongoing self-assessment, planning, and improvement initiatives.

Accreditation and Its Role in Higher Education

Accreditation was started in the nineteenth century to permit external control over educational standards (Selden, 1960). In the 1930s and 1940s, the North Central Association and Middle States Association added an emphasis on improvement. Middle States was the first to adopt a cycle of self-studies and visits from peers over a ten-year cycle (Selden, 1960). All regional accreditors now use the self-study and peer review process.

There are a total of six regional agencies across the United States that accredit higher education institutions in their particular area: New England, Middle States, Northwest, Western, North Central, and Southern. The system is voluntary. However, as of this writing, institutions must be accredited to ensure continued receipt of federal financial aid. This may not go on being the case because a bill was introduced in the last legislative session

NEW DIRECTIONS FOR INSTITUTIONAL RESEARCH, no. 123, Fall 2004   © Wiley Periodicals, Inc.

that would have removed the need for colleges to be accredited to receive federal student aid (Gose, 2002), and a report released earlier this year by the American Council of Trustees and Alumni advocated the same position (Eaton, 2002). In addition to regional accreditation, there are numerous discipline-specific accrediting agencies. This means that at any time an institution may be undergoing a self-study for institutional accreditation as well as one or more discipline-specific accreditations. The focus of this chapter is institutional-level accreditation.

True to its roots, accreditation still operates as a form of self-regulation. Four primary constituencies have a stake in accreditation: students, the higher education community as a whole, the public writ large, and federal and state governments (Eaton, 2001). Participation in accrediting activities offers several benefits for institutions beyond the obvious one of enabling eligibility for federal financial aid, most notably improvement and accountability.

Improvement. The process of conducting a self-assessment and hosting a peer review yields rich data for institutional improvement. This chapter uses the term *self-assessment* in place of the more commonly used phrase *self-study* to signify that current institutional accreditation standards have matured to the level where they now encourage measurement and analysis of institutional outcomes data. This replaces the former action of self-study, where resources and inputs were tabulated and few analyses were required. To conduct a self-assessment under current accreditation standards, substantial outcomes data and analyses are required. These data, when compared against accreditation standards, inevitably suggest improvement opportunities. Self-assessment is an opportunity for learning about the institution. The self-assessment team asks questions to increase their understanding of the current situation and trends, and this understanding can be used in turn to plan improvement opportunities.

Accountability to Students, the Public, and Government. When an institution is accredited, constituencies such as students, the public, and government representatives have at least some assurance of quality and value. It signifies that an institution meets the accreditation agency's standards and is accomplishing the goals it has set within the context of its mission. This assurance may in turn influence enrollment and funding decisions.

Renewal of Accreditation Standards

The reaccreditation system has been subject to criticism for some time; calls for greater accountability of higher education are loud and frequent. In response to these calls, accrediting agencies started proposing, as early as the late 1970s, a shift toward measuring performance in terms of outcomes rather than expenditures or resources (Bowen, 1979; Casey and Harris, 1979).

In recent years, there has been a national revision of standards toward institutional effectiveness with an emphasis on achievement of outcomes rather than adherence to standards. The most common suggestion for reform has been enhancement of internal mechanisms for quality assurance—in other words, the processes by which institutional effectiveness is ensured (Dill, Massy, Williams, and Cook, 1996). The criticism of earlier approaches was that they didn't compare outcomes with known approaches, and they didn't look at how data were used to guide decisions related to institutional effectiveness (Ewell, 1998). For example, Middle States is one of the regional accreditation agencies that have responded to the cry for revised standards; their new standards are described later in this chapter.

Institutional Effectiveness: Merging Accreditation, Planning, Assessment, and Improvement Initiatives

Many institutional planners and researchers emphasize the importance of relating planning and assessment initiatives in a continuous cycle to enhance institutional effectiveness. A few add improvement to the planning and assessment cycle in order to strengthen efforts toward institutional effectiveness. The model in Figure 2.1 displays one university's cycle of planning, assessment, and improvement that can be used by any office of planning or institutional research as it strives to support unit-level effectiveness initiatives. As we see later in this chapter and in the next one, such a systems model is akin to the quality improvement model used in the Baldrige process. Among the values implicit in this model are an emphasis on measurable outcomes, continuous improvement, using data in decision making, and involvement of internal and external stakeholders.

Current accreditation standards reflect many of these same values. It makes sense to integrate accreditation efforts with ongoing planning, assessment, and improvement initiatives. In fact, accreditation can be an important driver for assessment, planning, and improvement, and it may be cited as the reason for undertaking one or more of these initiatives. Accreditation standards now emphasize the assessment of student learning outcomes. Thus accreditation constitutes an important motivation to initiate outcomes assessment efforts. Many institutional research offices are already contributing to learning outcomes assessment and may also have the interest and ability to support accreditation efforts.

Accreditation standards can be used to guide assessment, planning, and resource allocation, and universities can look to these standards as representing best practices. Just as institutional mission and goals guide program development, resource allocation, and personnel decisions, they should guide an accreditation self-assessment. Accreditation is a potential input into strategic planning; institutional self-assessment is often used as a catalyst for strategic planning. Institutional performance data gathered for strategic planning are often used for self-assessment, and vice versa. The model in Figure 2.2 merges these ideas.

Figure 2.1. The Cycle of Planning, Assessment, and Improvement at Penn State University

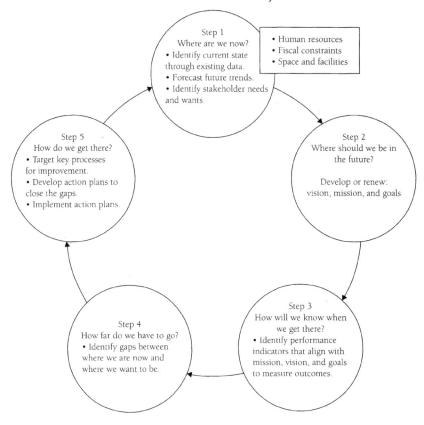

Step 1
Where are we now?
• Identify current state through existing data.
• Forecast future trends.
• Identify stakeholder needs and wants.

• Human resources
• Fiscal constraints
• Space and facilities

Step 2
Where should we be in the future?

Develop or renew:
vision, mission, and goals

Step 3
How will we know when we get there?
• Identify performance indicators that align with mission, vision, and goals to measure outcomes.

Step 4
How far do we have to go?
• Identify gaps between where we are now and where we want to be.

Step 5
How do we get there?
• Target key processes for improvement.
• Develop action plans to close the gaps.
• Implement action plans.

Source: Office of Planning and Institutional Assessment, Penn State University

This chapter proposes that achieving institutional effectiveness and accountability can be thought of as the final outcome from three processes:

1. Self-assessment and peer review
2. Planning
3. Learning outcomes assessment and program review

Inputs to this process include:

• Accreditation standards and other external influences
• The institution's mission and goals
• Data on student learning and other outcomes

Figure 2.2. A Model of Institutional Effectiveness That Integrates Accreditation, Planning, Assessment, and Improvement Initiatives

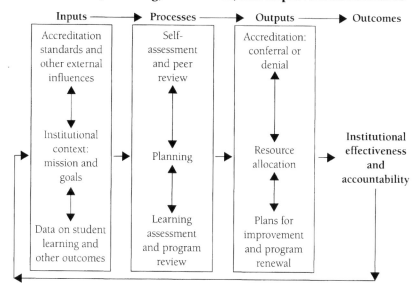

Among the outputs are:

- Accreditation conferral or denial
- Resource allocation
- Plans for improvement and program renewal

The model includes accreditation as an important part of the cycle of planning, assessment, and improvement. Together they maximize performance and produce effective and accountable organizations.

The Self-Study and Strategic Planning Processes

Let's consider how a college or university might integrate institutional accreditation into its planning, assessment, and improvement efforts to strengthen institutional effectiveness as it prepares for a self-study and site visit. It is not unreasonable to expect that, at least two years before the visit, the institution will appoint the leadership for the accreditation process and consider the type of self-study to be used (for example, comprehensive or selected topics). Within two years of the visit, the institution should initiate its self-assessment process. An internal steering committee and appropriate working groups are often appointed to ensure appropriate and effective participation from across the institution. By the time of the visit, these committees are involved in the processes of planning, compiling documentation, analyzing assessment data, drafting self-study report sections, and so on.

During a similar time frame, the planning or IR office can help ensure that strategic planning is used to inform the upcoming self-study. Each institution's situation is of course unique; however, a few possible ideas of how this can occur might be illustrative. If the institution has an established strategic planning process, communications such as planning guidelines or instructions to unit leaders should refer to appropriate aspects of the self-study. If the self-study report is to emphasize a theme such as assessing teaching and learning, or student services, or enrollment management, or resource allocation, the emphasis can be encouraged in planning and decision making. If significant new information gathering (perhaps a faculty and staff or student survey) would be useful, a time line of two to three years may not be unreasonable in terms of developing instruments, collecting data, analyzing and communicating results, and incorporating them into decision making. In short, the planning or IR office can look for various opportunities to help planning and accreditation activities complement one another, but adequate lead time is necessary.

Role of Institutional Research in Accreditation

The accreditation process comprises four steps:

1. Institutional self-assessment
2. Review team visit and written report
3. Institutional response
4. Agency action

Institutional research staff should be involved in most or all aspects of accreditation, starting with the self-assessment. Although the accreditation process officially ends (for at least two years) after agency notice is received, ideally the cycle of self-assessment, planning, and improvement will continue through the ensuing months and years. This cycle is informed by improvement opportunities uncovered by the self-assessment process; perhaps it is also informed by follow-up action required by the accrediting agency. As part of the agency action, an institution is often asked to prepare a two-year follow-up report that addresses suggestions and recommendations made by the review team. Institutional research staff are generally involved in coordinating or contributing to the follow-through on issues, suggestions, and recommendations.

Many IR offices are positioned to be the central point of contact for accreditation efforts, and certainly to be the clearinghouse for official data and information. Some offices are responsible for collecting assessment data, while others are responsible for reporting and disseminating results. Both sets of skills are needed for accreditation efforts. As self-assessment subcommittees form, they start discussing their data needs right away, so institutional research staff should be involved from the beginning. Institutional research staff members are often involved in data collection and reporting to support accountability efforts; therefore they may have the ability and interest to support an institution's accreditation process. Just as accountability measures are moving from emphasis on inputs to emphasis on outcomes, so are accreditation standards. It is important to know how to show the impact of what an institution does.

Self-Assessment Phase. Self-assessment is the most important part of the self-study process in terms of producing plans for improvement and program renewal that lead to institutional effectiveness and accountability. The self-assessment starts at least eighteen months before the review team's arrival, with a visit from a representative of the accrediting agency. This person explains that there are a variety of formats for the self-assessment, all of which respond to standards established by accreditors. The most common is the comprehensive approach, through which programs, services, and outcomes are studied in relation to the institution's goals and the agency's standards. The second most common format is the comprehensive approach with special emphases, which combines a shorter review of programs and outcomes with an in-depth assessment of topics of importance to the institution (such as general education and quality improvement processes). The third most common is the selected topics approach, in which one or more topics (for example, teaching and learning) are emphasized, with other standards described in the context of the topic(s) of focus (Kells, 1988).

Institutional research staff members often provide much of the data and analysis used as inputs into the processes of self-assessment, planning, learning outcomes assessment, and program review. They access individual- and unit-level data elements and create institutional summaries through aggregation. Of course, success in this effort demands foresight to anticipate the types of data needed. Much of the data on enrollment, faculty, and financial performance may be available through college or university data warehouses. Data on student learning outcomes and other performance outcomes may be more difficult to obtain, since these data rely on the participation of individuals and departments and often necessitate extra effort for collection. This is one area where institutional research staff may be instrumental in introducing methods to ease the work of collecting data that help document outcomes.

Visit from the Peer Review Team. Prior to the review team's arrival, institutional research staff may choose to set up a "document room" to house the supporting documentation requested by the team. In the Middle States region, the team arrives on a Sunday afternoon and leaves campus the following Wednesday. In that time, institutional research staff should expect to be on call at any time. The team inevitably has additional requests for data, and staff are expected to produce the information in a timely manner.

The review team is composed of peers; the institution has some say in who is on the review team. Stakeholders are not included on the review team. The president's or provost's office often coordinates logistics for the visit. Institutional research staff are likely to be in close contact with these offices during the visit.

The review team appraises elements of programs, services, and outcomes in relation to the institution's mission and goals. Their work is generally confined to interviews, document review, and direct observation. During the course of the team's data collection, they may informally make suggestions, so it is a good idea to listen carefully to their comments. The team works together each night during their visit; their report is substantially completed by the time they leave campus.

On the morning of the review team's final day of their visit, the chair of the team presents a verbal summary of the team's findings. Institutional research staff should be there to hear this report. Within two weeks, the institution receives the team's draft report for the purpose of checking its facts. Institutional research may be involved in this fact checking.

Three Frameworks for Self-Assessment

As mentioned earlier, there are six regional accreditation agencies in the United States. Their standards and approaches differ, but they all intend to promote institutional improvement and offer a means of demonstrating educational accountability. Among the regional agencies, the Middle States Association (MSA), North Central (NCA), and Western (WASC) agencies have led the accreditation effort to strengthen their standards and to require evidence of student learning outcomes as the central indicator of an educational institution's effectiveness. The Web sites of all accrediting agencies are indexed on the Association for Institutional Research (AIR) Web site (http://airweb.org/links/accred.cfm). The sites offer constructive frameworks on which to build an institution's accreditation and planning activities. We summarize three of them here: MSA, NCA, and Baldrige.

Middle States Commission on Higher Education. The Middle States' standards for accreditation are made up of fourteen items, half of which focus on institutional context and half on educational effectiveness. The 2002 edition of the standards is substantially revised, with greater emphasis on institutional assessment and learning outcomes assessment, and less emphasis on institutional resources and other input measures. These revisions suggest an even greater role for institutional research offices in completing the self-assessment since a higher volume of research and data analysis is needed to meet the standards related to institutional assessment and learning outcomes assessment. Further, once accredited an institution is expected to maintain ongoing self-assessment and improvement processes. The self-assessment process still includes a requirement for the institution to document how it meets the fourteen accreditation standards within the context of its own mission.

Here are the Middle States 2002 accreditation standards:

- Mission, goals, and objectives
- Planning, resource allocation, and institutional renewal
- Institutional resources
- Leadership and governance
- Administration
- Integrity
- Institutional assessment
- Student admissions
- Student support services
- Faculty
- Educational offerings
- General education
- Related educational activities
- Assessment of student learning

Detailed information on the fourteen MSA standards is in the handbook *Characteristics of Excellence in Higher Education* (2002). To illustrate the significant transition in standards, the 1994 standard on mission, goals, and objectives established a requirement for clearly stated mission and goals appropriate to the institution's resources and the needs of its constituents. The mission, goals, and objectives were to be clear, identifiable, honest, attainable, understood, used as a guide for thought and action, and stated in terms of results sought. In contrast, the 2002 standard for mission, goals, and objectives states that they guide "decisions related to planning, resource allocation, program and curriculum development, and definition of program outcomes." In addition, the document indicates that institutions are expected to have goals and objectives that focus on student learning outcomes and institutional improvement ("Characteristics of Excellence. . . . ," 2002, pp. 2–3). Moreover, standard fourteen spells out in some detail the MSA expectations for course level, program level, and institutional assessment evidence.

This example highlights just one of many areas where institutional research needs to play a much stronger role, since the standards now are much more focused on use of data to guide decisions and attainment of specific outcomes.

Malcolm Baldrige National Quality Award. The Baldrige quality award was established in 1988 to recognize and encourage performance excellence in the business sector. A decade later, award programs were established for both education and health care. Although fewer than one hundred organizations across all sectors apply for the award each year, hundreds of thousands of copies of the criteria are distributed yearly for use in organizational self-assessment. There are a number of higher education institutions using the Baldrige framework, or variations of it, for their own self-assessment, planning, and improvement purposes. In addition, regional

Figure 2.3. The Baldridge Criteria for Performance Excellence in Educational Organizations

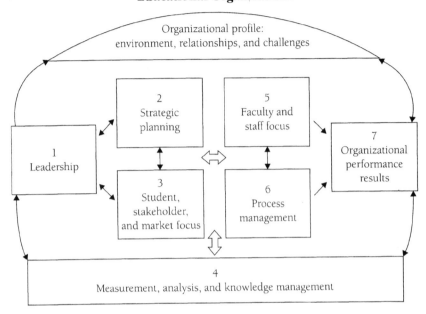

accrediting agencies are starting to allow use of the Baldrige criteria as an alternative accreditation format. North Central has modified the criteria to create its own customized accreditation quality assurance (described later).

The Baldrige criteria for education, like the traditional accreditation standards already discussed, emphasize learning outcomes. Other similarities are that both are designed to drive organizational improvement and both use the organization's mission and goals as the context. However, the similarities end there.

As shown in Figure 2.3, the Baldrige framework is a set of seven criteria linked in a fully interconnected, quality management system that supports and enhances institutional outcomes. It "fits together," meaning that all goals, measures, actions, and outcomes are linked. There is an emphasis on improvement trends, benchmarking, stakeholders, and learning outcomes. Categories one through three make up the leadership triad, defined as leadership (category one); strategic planning (category two); and student, stakeholder, and market focus (category three). The leadership triad links to the results triad, defined as faculty and staff focus (category five), process management (category six), and organizational performance results (category seven). Underlying these two integrated triads is a foundation of measurement, analysis, and knowledge management (category four). The organization's profile (mission, environment, and challenges) sets the context for the quality management system. Full integration of all seven criteria is arguably the most significant feature of the Baldrige criteria (see Figure 2.3). Traditional accreditation standards, though much improved, are at this time not linked to form a quality management system.

There are two other purposes for the criteria: to facilitate sharing best practices, and to serve as a tool for learning about and improving performance. Unlike traditional accreditation standards, the Baldrige criteria are not prescriptive. They focus on results rather than the specific procedures used to achieve them. This facilitates the ease with which colleges and universities can compare performance outcomes.

Institutional research staff may be most interested in category four: measurement, analysis, and knowledge management. Measurement and analysis are likely to be familiar tasks to many researchers, but sharing knowledge to enhance performance may be a new activity for an institutional research office. Category four examines selection, gathering, analysis, management, and improvement of data, information, and knowledge assets. Section 4.1, specifically, looks at measurement, analysis, alignment, and improvement of student and operational performance data and information at all levels and parts of the organization. Activities in this section are linked to categories one and two; performance results are reported in category seven. Section 4.2, on the other hand, focuses on how data and information are made available, and how organizational knowledge is collected and transferred.

The University of Wisconsin-Stout was a winner of the 2001 Malcolm Baldrige National Quality Award. It also participates in the AQIP accreditation program mentioned earlier in this chapter. Several research universities, notably Penn State, Rutgers, the University of California at Berkeley, and the University of Wisconsin-Madison, use a version of the Baldrige that was modified by Rutgers University to better serve large research universities. Entitled Excellence in Higher Education (EHE), it serves as a guide to institutional self-assessment, planning, and improvement (Ruben, 2001).

North Central Association of Colleges and Schools: AQIP. Using the Baldrige framework as a foundation, in 1999 the NCA, with the help of a Pew Charitable Trust grant, initiated an alternative format for institutions previously accredited under their traditional standards. By 2003, more than seventy institutions had participated in the Academic Quality Improvement Project (AQIP), among them Kent State, Ohio University, University of Wisconsin-Stout, and Purdue University (Gose, 2002). AQIP is modeled on the Malcolm Baldrige National Quality Award, modified for higher education as described previously. Institutions using AQIP for reaccreditation maintain a portfolio, of no more than one hundred pages, documenting their ongoing progress on the nine AQIP criteria:

1. Helping students learn
2. Accomplishing other distinctive objectives

3. Understanding students' and other stakeholders' needs
4. Valuing people
5. Leading and communicating
6. Supporting institutional operations
7. Measuring effectiveness
8. Planning continuous improvement
9. Building collaborative relationships

The nine AQIP criteria differ in many ways from traditional accreditation standards. Perhaps most notably, they are nonprescriptive, focus on both process and results, and emphasize continuous improvement. In other words, for each criterion the institution describes its processes, deployment, and results, as well as how it is using performance data to drive improvement. Participants do say that the AQIP process takes more time than self-assessment for traditional reaccreditation, but it holds greater long-term value thanks to significant emphasis on continuous improvement and systems thinking (Newton, 2002).

Institutional research staff in institutions that are considering AQIP involvement can expect to be called on to manage or assist in the process of establishing and maintaining the one-hundred-page portfolio that documents progress on the nine criteria. More information on AQIP is available at http://www.aqip.org.

Conclusion

This chapter reviews the importance of accreditation to higher education and outlines the role of institutional research in the reaccreditation cycle. Institutional research plays a lead role in an integrated approach to institutional effectiveness where accreditation activities are fully linked to ongoing planning, self-assessment, and improvement initiatives. Figures 2.1, 2.2, and 2.3 display three models illustrating these linkages and cycles.

Recently revised standards by such regional accreditation agencies as Middle States, North Central, and Western have significantly increased the amount and types of data collection and analysis required for the self-assessment that is part of the reaccreditation cycle. Thus the role for institutional research offices in accreditation is likely to broaden.

Institutional research offices have traditionally furnished data to support university decision making, and many also have provided data used for accountability reporting. Now that regional accreditors are focusing on measurement of outcomes and use of outcomes data to make decisions that enhance institutional effectiveness, it is important for researchers to strengthen their understanding of the bigger picture of institutional effectiveness and how the various processes can be linked. Through an understanding of these potential linkages, accreditation can become a catalyst for institutional effectiveness. Further, institutional researchers can introduce leaders to complementary self-assessment frameworks, such as the Baldrige criteria or the Excellence in Higher Education criteria, so that IR can be used to stimulate ongoing effectiveness, even when not actively conducting a reaccreditation self-assessment.

References

Bowen, H. R. "Outcomes Assessment: A New Era in Accreditation." Paper presented at the Annual Convention of the Middle States Association of Colleges and Schools, Dec. 5–7, 1979.

Casey, R. J., and Harris, J. W. *Accountability in Higher Education: Forces, Counterforces, and the Role of Institutional Accreditation.* Washington, D.C.: Council on Postsecondary Accreditation, 1979.

"Characteristics of Excellence in Higher Education: Eligibility Requirements and Standards for Accreditation." 2002, http://www.msache.org; retrieved Apr. 3, 2003.

Dill, D. D., Massy, W. F., Williams, P. R., and Cook, C. M. "Accreditation and Academic Quality Assurance." *Change,* 1996, *28,* 17–24.

Eaton, J. S. "Regional Accreditation Reform: Who Is Served?" *Change,* 2001, *33,* 39–45.

Eaton, J. S. "Before You Bash Accreditation, Consider the Alternatives." *Chronicle of Higher Education,* 2002, *49*(25).http://chronicle.com/weekly/v49/i25/25b01501.htm; retrieved Feb. 27, 2003.

Ewell, P. T. "Examining a Brave New World: How Accreditation Might Be Different." Paper presented at the Council for Higher Education Accreditation "Usefulness" Conference, Washington, D.C., June 25–26, 1998.

Gose, B. "A Radical Approach to Accreditation: Can the Academic Quality Improvement Project Make the Process Worth the Time and Money?" *Chronicle of Higher Education,* 2002, *49*(10). http://chronicle.com/weekly/v49/i10/10a02502.htm; retrieved Nov. 4, 2002.

Kells, H. R. *Self-Study Processes: A Guide for Postsecondary and Similar Service-Oriented Institutions and Programs* (3rd ed.). New York: Macmillan, 1988.

Newton, K. "New Frontiers in Regional Accreditation: AQIP Is Here." Paper presented at the annual conference of the National Consortium for Continuous Improvement annual conference, Vancouver. B.C., Canada, July 2002.

Ruben, B. D. *Excellence in Higher Education 2001–2002: A Baldrige-Based Guide to Organizational Assessment, Planning and Improvement.* Washington, D.C.: National Association of College and University Business Officers, 2001.

Selden, W. K. *Accreditation: A Struggle over Standards in Higher Education.* New York: HarperCollins, 1960.

Ann H. Dodd is assistant dean and senior research associate in the College of Agricultural Sciences at Penn State University. She is an evaluator for the Middle States Commission on Higher Education and was an examiner for the 2000 Malcolm Baldrige National Quality Award.

3

This chapter extends the discussion of the Baldrige framework in the preceding chapter by highlighting the eleven lessons learned from Baldrige best-practice organizations.

Strategic Planning via Baldrige: Lessons Learned

John Jasinski

The Malcolm Baldrige National Quality Award program, signed into law in 1987, is internationally recognized for its promotion of performance excellence practices within the education, health care, and business sectors. The award is named after the late Malcolm Baldrige, the U.S. Secretary of Commerce from 1981–1987, because in large part "Baldrige was a proponent of quality management as a key to this country's prosperity and long-term strength."[1] The program's original intent and ongoing focus is to recognize role model organizations for quality and performance excellence, and to promote dialogue within and among the education, health care, and business sectors regarding national competitiveness issues of quality and performance excellence. The Council on Competitiveness suggests the Baldrige program has made quality a key focal point for America and its organizations by virtue of recognizing performance excellence and sharing best practices.[2]

The National Institute of Standards and Technology in the U.S. Department of Commerce manages the program with the combined help of a public-private partnership involving a foundation, the American Society for Quality, a board of overseers, a board of examiners, and current and past award recipients. The mutual efforts of these organizations help fulfill the program's mission of recognition and sharing.

The Baldrige program uses a set of nonprescriptive criteria that David Garvin of the Harvard Business School has said offer a "comprehensive framework for assessing progress toward the new paradigm of management."[3] The balanced and holistic Baldrige criteria support a systems perspective and a focus on results. These are the overall purposes of the Baldrige Criteria:

- Helping improve organizational performance practices, capabilities, and results
- Facilitating communication and sharing of best-practices information among U.S. organizations of all types
- Serving as a working tool for understanding and improving performance and for guiding planning and opportunities for learning[4]

The Baldrige program, then, focuses on learning and sharing, not just on winning an award. Learning comes through application and assessment using the criteria, which are updated annually for the education, health care, and business sectors (at the time of this writing, legislation is pending in Congress to extend the Baldrige program into the not-for-profit sector as well). The *2004 Education Criteria for Performance Excellence* (http://www. quality.nist.gov) are based on a set of interrelated core values and concepts (visionary leadership; learning-centered education; organizational and personal learning; valuing faculty, staff, and partners; agility; focus on the future; managing for innovation; management by fact; social responsibility; focus on results and creating value; and systems perspective). Organizations of varying types and sizes use the Baldrige criteria and its systems-based framework to drive improvement efforts by addressing questions within the seven cross-cutting categories (see Figure 2.3, in the preceding chapter). Baldrige actively facilitates sharing through numerous forums, chief among them the annual Quest for Excellence (QE) Conference.[5] The QE highlights award recipients' best practices across the seven categories. Within the past two years, eight diverse organizations have received recognition as Baldrige Award recipients. One higher education, two K–12, one health care, two small business, and two manufacturing organizations have been recognized as role models and asked to share their stories and experiences.

This chapter focuses on Baldrige category two (strategic planning and high-level learning) and extracts the key lessons learned from these eight organizations. The diversity of these eight recognized organizations and the lessons learned can serve as models for higher education strategic planning improvement. Baldrige category two addresses strategic planning by asking institutions a series of *how* and *what* questions regarding strategy development processes, strategic objectives, action plan development and deployment, and performance projection. These eleven lessons learned represent common themes across the eight model organizations.

1. Strategic planning best practices begin with a clear map of the organization's strategic planning process. This includes key steps, key participants, short- and long-term planning time horizons, how horizons are set, and how organizations incorporate these horizons into their planning process. The norm for the eight organizations is a clear visual depiction—usually a process flowchart of some sort—depicting key steps.

2. Strategic planning operates on a closed–loop cycle. Practices entail monthly or quarterly steps, outlined quite specifically and owned by a range of leaders within an organization. The ongoing cycle includes, for example, regular periodic reviews of an organization's mission, vision, and values and specific phases for plan development, deployment, reporting, and adjustment.

3. Organizations systematically collect and analyze numerous inputs as feeders into their strategy development. These inputs may range from data and information regarding technological changes to an assessment of strengths and weaknesses; or from risk assessments and gap analyses to changes in the local, regional, national, and international environments. In essence, an organization builds forecasts and scenarios on systematically gathered, defined, and reviewed internal and external scans.

4. Organizations identify a manageable number of strategic objectives (perhaps four to six), tied to inputs that systematically address the major challenges they face. These strategic objectives cover both short- and long-term horizons and balance the key needs of students and stakeholders. These eight organizations share the common trait of establishing specific goals for the strategic objectives and identify key owners to help carry out deployment and execution of the objectives and goals.

5. Organizations specify a deployment plan to achieve the strategic objectives, including a step for resource allocation. Deployment methods vary, but the norm for these eight organizations involves cascading deployment across all organizational levels. Similar to plan development, plan deployment is an ongoing process of (1) regular progress checks and methods of reporting for individual objectives and overall strategy progress, and (2) celebration of progress. Given that a mere 15 percent of Fortune 500 CEOs cite success in executing their business strategy, successful strategy deployment appears to be a clear differentiating factor in organizational success.[6]

6. Benchmarks are used to report and analyze progress on action plans designed to meet strategic objectives. Organizations track key performance measures and indicators, project short- and long-term performance, and track current and projected future performance against comparative and competitive benchmark organizations. Each organization typically uses relevant benchmark comparative data from outside its own industry to help drive breakthrough improvements.

7. Strategic planning best practices include a clear linkage between human resource plans and strategic objectives and action plans. Human resource plans typically cover areas such as recruitment, retention, development, and succession issues. Beyond the human resource component, technology plans, academic plans, an organization's performance measurement system, and the like align with and integrate into strategic objectives and action plans. Overall strategic plans, then, link to all levels of an organization.

8. Another norm for the eight organizations is that they dedicate annually a given time period (for example, one or two days, or a week) every six months to focus on strategic planning activities. During this time, for example, a review of the planning process, analysis of inputs, review of key performance results, alteration of strategic objectives, and so on occurs.

9. As an organization takes its pulse via systematic strategic planning processes, it simultaneously builds an evaluation and improvement cycle within. This facilitates more rapid maturity of its planning process and likewise achieves results. Evaluation and improvement methodologies vary but typically entail a combination of formative and summative analyses, internal and external planning process and performance checks, and formal and informal methods.

10. These eight model organizations use performance results to help build and execute strategy. A clear line of sight exists along an organization's strategy development, deployment, leadership decision making, and organizational performance. As such, higher education organizations factor in the results of organizational effectiveness; student, faculty, and staff performance; social responsibility; governance and stakeholder influence; and budgetary, financial, and market trends.

11. Line-of-sight clarity extends to an open, intentional, and structured communication framework regarding organizational strategy. Such communication appears to be a key component of successful strategy deployment; the common lesson learned is that communication focuses on both simplicity and rapidity of messaging.

In sum, Baldrige best-practice organizations address common planning mechanisms found in many higher education institutions. However, as the evidence shows these eight Baldrige-honored organizations promote and execute systematic approaches nuanced by organizational culture and mission. The *hows* can vary across organizational type, but the nonnegotiable keys to sustained success adhere to the lessons I have noted. These important and interconnected lessons are shared among organizations in higher education and other sectors. As such, a golden opportunity exists for institutions of higher learning to heighten the usefulness of these lessons by using the Baldrige criteria and by learning and sharing with other institutions.

Notes

1. Frequently Asked Questions about the Malcolm Baldrige National Quality Award, n.d. (http://www.nist.gov/public_affairs/factsheet/baldfaqs.htm).
2. Council on Competitiveness. "Building on Baldrige: American Quality for the 21st Century." Washington, D.C.: Council on Competitiveness, July 1995.
3. Garvin, D. A. "How the Baldrige Award Really Works." *Harvard Business Review,* Nov.–Dec. 1991.
4. Baldrige National Quality Program. *2004 Education Criteria for Performance Excellence.* 2004 (http://www.quality.nist.gov).

5. All references used in this chapter, unless otherwise indicated, were accessed via Quest for Excellence XIV (2002) and XV (2003) proceedings. For further information on award recipients encompassing the Baldrige program's history, see http://www.quality.nist.gov or e-mail the Baldrige National Quality Program at nqp@nist.gov.
6. Charan, R., and Colvin, G. "Why CEO's Fail." *Fortune,* June 21, 1999, p. 70.

JOHN JASINSKI is the principal of Jasinski Consulting Services in Maryville, Missouri.

Environmental scanning, enrollment forecasting, budget analyses, and institutional effectiveness assessment are examples of the explicit contributions institutional research offices make to campus strategic planning.

Applying Ad Hoc Institutional Research Findings to College Strategic Planning

Craig A. Clagett

Throughout this volume, the authors emphasize that institutional research is integral to effective planning. This chapter poses a new twist by giving examples of institutional research projects that were undertaken for reasons other than strategic planning that nevertheless had a profound influence on planning efforts. The research was instrumental in (1) defining and explaining student achievement, (2) designing a student fee structure, and (3) defusing a hot political issue. Although the usefulness of the research findings for planning eventually became apparent, the studies initially were *ad hoc* and reactive.

The case studies summarized here, although from community colleges, are applicable to institutions of all types. The lessons they convey may serve as models for successful research applications in other settings. Nevertheless, while reviewing these cases the reader will want to keep in mind that despite having much in common with other segments of higher education, community colleges are distinctive in their emphasis on access—academic, financial, geographic, and temporal access—and their focus on local economic development.

Case Studies of the Impact of Institutional Research on College Planning

The three cases presented here demonstrate some ways that institutional research can contribute to college planning, beyond environmental scanning and enrollment forecasting. In each example, the institutional research was initiated for purposes other than strategic planning. Data were generated to answer questions about student achievement and high tuition, to address a fiscal crisis, and to defuse a hot political situation. In the end, however, the research influenced strategic planning at the respective colleges with lasting impact. Years after their completion, the studies continue to live on in fee structures and current strategic planning initiatives, thus leaving an institutional research legacy.

Example One: Defining Student Achievement in Community Colleges

By emphasizing opportunity through open-admissions policies, community colleges encourage higher learning among many students lacking the basic skills, study habits, and support networks that facilitate success. As a result, community colleges often fare poorly on traditional assessment measures such as graduation rate. Accrediting agencies, state oversight boards, legislators, and the public media focus attention on these poor performance comparisons and on the high need for academic remediation among community college students. To meet statutory reporting mandates, accreditation requirements, and public relations needs, colleges increasingly turn to their institutional research offices to conduct analytical studies of student performance and other outcomes. This is especially true for institutions serving diverse populations (Keeton, Engleberg, and Clagett, 1998). Many community college students are the first in their family to attend college, making the transition to college complex and challenging.

Among nontraditional, primarily first-generation college students, however, the adaptation to college was far more difficult. Indeed, for many going to college constituted a major *disjunction* in their life course. For these students, college going was not part of the family's tradition or expectations; on the contrary. Those who were the first in their immediate family to attend college were *breaking,* not continuing, family tradition. For these students, college attendance often involved multiple transitions—academic, social, and cultural (Terenzini and others, 1994).

Committed to their mission, most community colleges continuously strive to ease these transitions and promote student persistence and achievement. This case study describes institutional research efforts in the 1990s to understand student performance at Prince George's Community College (PGCC), a relatively large (fall headcount twelve thousand), diverse (70 percent minority), suburban community college in Maryland (Clagett, 1996). Two-fifths of the students attending the college were the first in their family to do so.

In response to external accountability demands and internal decision support needs, the college's office of institutional research developed longitudinal student tracking files to facilitate student achievement studies. An outcomes typology was created that (1) was comprehensible and accepted as legitimate by various stakeholders; (2) took into account the full range of student goals for attending college; (3) acknowledged student enrollment behavior patterns, including part-time and stop-out attendance; and (4) permitted a summary of student accomplishment useful to campus policy makers.

Given the nature of the community college mission, outcomes measures should differ from those developed for four-year institutions (Pascarella, Smart, and Ethington, 1986; Webb, 1989; Seppanen, 1995). For example, an analysis of time to degree of 1,581 associate degree graduates of the City Colleges of Chicago found that nearly a fifth took ten years or more to finish their "two-year" degree. Nearly a fourth of the total time to degree for this cohort was accounted for by stop-out time (elapsed while the students were not enrolled). Most notably, nearly half the time to degree was accounted for by "extra time enrolled," beyond the nominal requirements for the degree. This extra time was due to part-time attendance, time spent earning credits not needed for the associate's degree, and time spent in classes not completed. Noncredit remedial courses accounted for 6 percent of the extra time (Garcia z, 1994).

With these issues in mind, the college's research office developed eight student outcomes categories that were based on the data available in its longitudinal cohort tracking system (Clagett, 1995):

1. *Award and transfer.* The percentage of degree-seeking students in an entering cohort who earned a degree or certificate from the college *and* transferred to a four-year institution within the study period.

2. *Transfer or no award.* The percentage of degree-seeking students transferring to a senior institution without having earned an award from the college.

3. *Award or no transfer.* The percentage of degree-seeking students earning a degree or certificate from the college for whom there is no evidence of transfer.

4. *Sophomore status in good standing.* The percentage of degree-seeking students who have not graduated from the college but who have earned at least thirty credits with a cumulative grade point average of 2.0 or above, and for whom there was no evidence of transfer. Given the proportion of entering students needing remediation or attending part-time, reaching sophomore status in good standing represents a notable academic achievement.

5. *Achievers.* A summary measure of the preceding four categories.

6. *Persisters.* The percentage of degree-seeking students still enrolled at the college (as of the last term of the study period) who do not fall into any of the achiever categories.

7. *Nonachievers.* The percentage of degree-seeking students exiting the college without graduating or earning thirty credits in good standing for whom there was no evidence of transfer. This group includes true dropouts,

stop-outs, and some students who may have transferred before accumulating thirty credits.

8. *Special motive.* Students who indicated short-term, nondegree goals of personal enrichment or job skill upgrading *and* who attended only during the first two terms of the study period. Never intending to enter a curriculum or transfer, these students are properly excluded from attrition statistics.

These classifications become most meaningful when a substantial majority of the cohort have attained their ultimate desired outcome. Although this argues for a fairly long study period (say, six years or more), another consideration supports a shorter time span. Reporting on cohorts that entered sometime ago runs the risk that student characteristics and institutional practices may have changed, such that the findings may not be a useful guide for current policy making. This study reported the achievements of students four years after they entered the college as freshmen in the fall of 1990 (Boughan and Clagett, 1995) and demonstrated how the findings subsequently influenced strategic planning.

A total of 2,643 first-time students entered the college in fall 1990. Of these, 257 were enrolled for short-term enrichment or specific skill upgrading and indicated that they had no intention of earning credits toward a degree. Among the 2,386 degree-seeking students, 137 (fewer than 6 percent) had been awarded a degree from the college by the end of spring 1994. Another 214 (or 9 percent) transferred to a four-year in-state public college. Thus, after four years, nearly 15 percent had earned a degree or transferred. An additional 314 students, or 13 percent, had earned at least thirty credits at the college with a cumulative grade point average of 2.0 or above. Including these sophomores in good standing with the graduates and transfers, the total proportion of fall 1990 entrants classified as achievers within four years was 28 percent. Thus, even with a lenient definition of achievement, fewer than a third of the students were successful four years after their entry as first-time students.

The next step involved examining student patterns of attendance to see if they were associated with student outcomes. Students attending in fall 1990 and for at most only one other term were unlikely to attain achiever status. Only 4 percent of these short-term attendees were classified as achievers, most through transfer to a senior institution. Among those students attending at least three terms, however, a substantial difference was found. Students who attended the first three major terms (fall 1990, spring 1991, and fall 1991) were more than twice as likely to be achievers as students who were absent in either spring or fall 1991. A majority (54 percent) of those getting off to a "good start" had graduated, transferred, or attained sophomore status in good standing within four years of entry, compared to only 22 percent of those who attended three or more terms but did not enroll in all of the first three major terms. Students with the good start—enrolling in at least the first three terms without interruption—had higher rates of graduation, transfer, and sophomore attainment.

Achievement level varied with the number of skill areas needing remediation. Students who were college-ready and did not need remediation had an achievement rate of 45 percent. Twenty-eight percent of the students needing remediation in one basic skill graduated, transferred, or attained sophomore status in good standing within four years of entry. The achievement rate dropped to 17 percent for those needing developmental classes in two areas, and 11 percent for those needing developmental classes in all three areas of mathematics, reading, and composition.

Achievement rate was calculated for several academic variables, each of which appeared to be associated with student success. The more terms a student attended, and the more credits carried each term, the higher the achievement. Students who attended without interruption had a higher achievement rate; those who were always in good academic standing had a higher achievement rate than those who attended one or more terms on academic probation or restriction. In reality, of course, the factors inhibiting or facilitating academic success are cumulative and interactive.

The findings from the longitudinal cohort analyses guided the planning efforts of a subsequently appointed Campus Retention Committee. The research findings clearly influenced the committee, as reflected in their final recommendations, summarized here (Campus Retention Committee, 1996). Note how often explicit research findings are referenced.

- *Improve developmental student success.* Campus research suggests that students who complete all required developmental courses achieve *at the same rate* as students entering the college without basic skill deficiencies. However, research shows that relatively few students identified as needing developmental education succeed in completing remediation. The Campus Retention Committee believes that assisting students through completion of all developmental requirements should be a top priority.
- *Initiate or expand departmental retention programs.* Campus research shows that student success varies by student major and by course discipline. An academic department should establish retention programs tailored to its discipline and the goals of the students. The department might focus on courses with a low student pass rate, on the appropriateness of placement test score requirements, and on the effectiveness of 100-level preparatory courses. The department should annually report on the nature and success of its programs to the Campus Retention Committee.
- *Expand early intervention programs.* Institutional research confirms the importance of a good start in college. The sooner academic difficulties are identified and interventions initiated, the greater the likelihood of student success. The early alert program should be expanded to include personal follow-up contacts with all identified students. The system should alert intervention teams as well as the student; the institution should be

obligated to implement intervention programs once students in academic trouble are identified.

• *Increase faculty involvement in student support services.* The Campus Retention Committee believes that the college should train and use more faculty members in registration, ongoing student advisement, college activities, mentoring programs, high school recruitment, and other student support activities. The national literature and findings from the evaluation of the college's mentoring program suggest that student-faculty interactions outside the classroom promote student commitment and persistence.

• *Provide tuition scholarship aid to achieving, part-time students.* Campus research shows that many high-achieving students (grade point average of 3.0 and above) discontinue their studies, in many cases because of financial difficulties. Research also shows that students who "stop out" succeed at one-fourth the rate of those who continue their studies without interruption. The Campus Retention Committee recommends that financial assistance be targeted to part-time, employed adult students with a proven PGCC course history who are facing financial barriers to uninterrupted enrollment.

• *Improve student orientation to college.* Research shows that more than a fourth of the students entering the college each fall do not return for a second term. The Campus Retention Committee recommends revision of the college's program for assisting students in their transition to college, including better promotional campaigns to inform students about the support programs available, the success of students who complete developmental studies, and the advantages of remaining at PGCC through degree completion. The college should investigate the effectiveness of the CAP 102 course on achieving college success, and it should consider the merits of a similar one-credit college transition and orientation class to serve a broader range and larger number of students.

The spirit of the retention committee's recommendations resonate with sentiments expressed by Terenzini and colleagues (1994):

> In the past, we have tended to develop new student support programs implicitly assuming that the challenge is to help students adapt to the institution. For nontraditional and diverse students, however, the logic needs to be reversed: Institutions must seek ways in which *they* can change so as to accommodate the transitional and learning needs of first-generation and other nontraditional students. Some students will flourish in their new environment without institutional intervention. Others, however, will require assistance that is initiated by institutional representatives—faculty and staff. Faculty cannot assume that their sole responsibility is to teach and advise, and that if students do not take advantage of what they have to offer it is the student's problem. The burden of responsibility for taking advantage of transition support mechanisms cannot rest with the student alone [p. 72].

This view became the guiding philosophy of strategic planning at the college. Here are lessons for institutional researchers learned from this case study:

- *Design assessment measures appropriate to institutional mission and clientele.* Given the short study period imposed on most research, defining achievement as attaining sophomore status in good standing accommodated the realities of this community college.
- *Drill down to uncover policy-relevant findings.* Examine correlates of success, and start the journey by addressing the *why* questions. This means more difficult and time-consuming studies, but the investment is the only way to develop data to support policy prescriptions that have a hope of making a difference.
- *Welcome opportunities to serve on a committee where research can influence policy.* This makes the profession rewarding and worthwhile.

Example Two: Designing a Student Fee Structure to Raise Revenue

As colleges introduce programs to meet local and regional employment demand, the issue of how to pay for them surfaces. This is particularly challenging when new programs are inherently more expensive than existing curricula. Particularly in the nursing and allied health professions, mandated clinical requirements may impose a low student-faculty ratio and laboratory classes may involve expensive equipment and supplies. Carroll Community College, a relatively young and growing institution, faced this situation in 2002.

When the cost of offering programs varies, a question arises as to whether students enrolling in more expensive disciplines should pay more. If all students pay the same, regardless of the costs associated with the courses they choose, students in less expensive disciplines may be subsidizing those in more expensive disciplines. A differential fee structure could address this potential inequity and raise the additional revenue needed to fund the expensive new programs.

What is a discipline-based fee structure? Most colleges charge fees in addition to tuition. Fees are imposed for a variety of reasons, such as covering instructional costs not paid by tuition. A discipline-based fee structure addresses additional instructional costs. Colleges and universities typically collect instructional fees in one of two ways: through specific fees associated with individual courses, or through a consolidated fee sometimes calculated as a percentage of the tuition bill. A discipline-based fee structure falls in the middle; fees are associated with disciplines (English, mathematics, sociology) rather than individual courses.

Why not have a separate fee for courses in each discipline, on the basis of the historical costs of teaching? In the past, it was common practice to have fees associated with individual courses. Some college catalogues had a long listing of individual course fees. The fees varied widely, from as little as $2.00 per course to several hundred dollars. It was difficult for students to estimate their bills. The fact that a majority of courses might have fees, that the fees varied from course to course, and that the fee information was not easily accessible often created the perception of "hidden fees" that was much resented by students.

Further, the actual costs of delivering a particular course may vary from year to year, depending on changes in faculty assignment and class enrollment. Aggregating costs to the discipline level can reduce this year-to-year variability, yielding a more stable per-student cost that can more readily justify a tiered fee structure.

Have other colleges implemented a discipline-based fee structure? Yes. Maryland's Prince George's Community College (the first case study in this chapter) is one. PGCC implemented a discipline-cost-based "instructional services fee" (ISF) as part of its response to the budget shortfalls associated with the 1991–92 recession (Clagett, 1994).

A discipline-cost-analysis system developed by the Maryland State Board of Community Colleges in 1973 set the foundation for the new fee structure. The SBCC program yielded total cost per FTE student for teaching classes in each instructional discipline. The discipline cost analysis had been completed annually for nearly two decades, so the college felt confident about results that were based on years of refining the analysis, and extensive trend data. The analysis documented a stable difference in per-student costs across disciplines. For example, in 1993 management courses cost $3,293 per FTE, chemistry $4,893, and nuclear medicine technology $7,118.

It was deemed essential to base the new fees on actual cost data. This furnished the rationale and justification for imposition of higher costs on students.

What does a discipline-based fee structure look like? PGCC implemented a three-tiered fee structure, according to actual per-student costs by discipline and roughly corresponding to predominant instructional teaching method: level one ($15 per credit hour) disciplines were typically taught in lecture classes, level two ($20 per credit hour) usually used laboratories, and level three ($25 per credit hour) comprised limited-enrollment health technology courses.

When the ISF was introduced, 70 percent of the college's annual credit hours were in level one disciplines, 27 percent in level two, and 3 percent in level three. The new fee structure cost a part-time student carrying seven credit hours an additional $91 to $136 per term, depending on the particular courses taken. Despite the higher cost to students associated with the ISF, enrollment in health technology disciplines at PGCC increased steadily after implementation of the new fee structure.

Are there any other advantages of a tiered, discipline-based fee structure? A tiered instructional services fee structure built on discipline costs can be an efficient management tool in times of changing costs, teaching methods, and programming. As an existing discipline moves from a predominantly classroom-lecture pedagogy to computer-centered instruction, for example, its average class size may fall and associated costs may rise. If the discipline cost analysis shows this to be the case, the discipline can be moved from level one to level two of the fee structure. This is an easy, administrative way to generate additional revenue to cover the increased costs. When a new program and its associated courses are introduced, it is assigned to the fee level on the basis of its estimated costs. If subsequent discipline cost analyses warrant it, the discipline can be moved to another fee level to better balance costs and revenues.

Discipline-based, tiered fee structures can be simpler to understand and administer than course-based fees. When Prince George's implemented its ISF, three fee levels replaced 271 separate course fees.

What are the disadvantages of a discipline-based fee structure? At a college without individual course fees, students pay the same regardless of the course or discipline in which they enroll. A nursing student pays the same rate as an accounting student. A discipline-cost-based fee structure alters this, so that some students pay more than others for the same course load. If these differential fees are tied to instructional costs, the argument can be made that this is more equitable than the "all students pay the same" approach. But it is still the case that a student taking seven hours may pay an amount different from what another student taking seven hours pays, if they are enrolled in disciplines having different fees. To some, this seems unfair.

A greater concern is the potential disincentive associated with higher cost. With discipline-based fee structures, all courses in a discipline have the same fee. For example, nursing students pay at this higher fee rate for all of their nursing courses. Accumulated across all required courses in the program, this raises the cost of a nursing degree substantially over the cost of a program with a lower associated discipline fee. To the extent that this higher cost persuades students to avoid nursing and choose a less-expensive major, the discipline-based fee structure is problematic. With high-cost programs, enrollment at capacity is desirable to maximize revenue and reduce per-student costs.

Introduction of a differential, cost-based fee structure requires a clear marketing message, explaining the rationale and justification for new fees. Since the introduction of high-cost programs is usually associated with strong employment demand, marketing efforts might include information about the positive career prospects associated with program completion. A high-cost program may be a terrific value if it prepares students for well-paying and satisfying jobs.

A discipline cost analysis must be conducted regularly to verify that disciplines are appropriately placed in fee levels. This is important since the public justification for imposing the differential fees is the variation in costs of delivering instruction across disciplines.

Does the predominant teaching mode (lecture, laboratory, clinical setting) influence per-student course delivery costs? The variance in the cost of delivering courses is often associated with the nature of the instruction. Programs with required clinical experiences typically have a low, mandated student-faculty ratio (such as a maximum of eight students per instructor). Laboratory-intensive courses may have limited seat capacity in addition to expenses associated with laboratory equipment and supplies. Thus it is not unusual for a clinical or laboratory course to be more expensive per student than a lecture-based class. Studies at other institutions have commonly found nursing courses to be more expensive than chemistry courses, which are more expensive than sociology courses.

What other factors may contribute to differing per-student costs of delivering courses? The instructional delivery mode is not the only source of variance in per-student costs. Studies have identified a number of factors associated with varying discipline costs, including (1) the proportion of sections taught by adjunct as opposed to full-time faculty, (2) the proportion of faculty in higher ranks (full professors as opposed to assistant professors or lecturers). and (3) average class size. A discipline with few adjuncts and whose full-time faculty have reached higher ranks is substantially more expensive than a discipline taught in a similar way but by a large cadre of adjuncts or full-time faculty at the beginning of their career. Other things equal, it is more expensive (per student) to deliver a discipline with a relatively low average class size than a discipline with larger classes.

It is important to have faculty workload and class size data available to help interpret variations in discipline costs per student. An understanding of the factors accounting for differing discipline per-student costs helps justify assignment to fee level. If a particularly high (or low) cost-per-FTE in a given year simply reflects an aberration in the normal faculty assignments in the discipline (for example, the ratio of full-time to adjunct or the number of sections taught by full professors changes because of sabbaticals or released-time projects), no change in fee level may be warranted. In contrast, if a policy decision to reduce class size or introduce or expand laboratory requirements is raising costs, a fee level move may be appropriate.

What analysis needs to be done to make a wise decision about a discipline-cost-based, tiered fee structure? An informed choice requires two key steps: first, completing a discipline cost analysis, and then developing a scenario analysis that explores the likely impact of various combinations of discipline charges and fee levels on enrollments and revenues.

To sum up: the policy issue for the college was the desirability of introducing a new fee structure to raise needed revenue to fund new programs. The specific proposal investigated was a multitiered, discipline-grouped fee that is based on historical differences in instructional costs. Institutional research was charged with two tasks: conducting the cost analysis and clarifying policy issues for the board of trustees. The preceding narrative is how the latter task was accomplished.

Here are lessons for institutional research that were learned from this case study:

• First, *clear exposition of policy options and their underlying value judgments* can be an important contribution of institutional research. Research is more than data.

• Second, *literature reviews, Internet inquiries, and Web searches to identify best practices* as possible models for campus adoption can be a valuable contribution of institutional research. Again, research is more than data.

Example Three: Defusing an Emotional Financial and Political Issue

Perhaps the most challenging ad-hoc research projects take place within a highly charged political environment. Racially tinged charges of tuition gouging were hurled at Prince George's Community College in the early 1990s; this was a prime example of the political value of institutional research.

Community colleges in Maryland receive financial support from both state and local jurisdictions (Baltimore City Community College, a state-supported institution, is an exception). Each college has a local board of trustees empowered to set tuition and fees. Thanks to differences in county funding support, demographics, and political culture, the tuition and fees charged by Maryland's community colleges vary substantially. PGCC historically had one of the highest tuition rates in Maryland.

The college serves a large suburban county bordering the nation's capital. Driven mostly by in-migration from the district and out-migration to neighboring Maryland counties, Prince George's County's African American population almost quadrupled, from 14 percent to 51 percent from 1970 to 1990. Newly elected county officials turned their attention to PGCC's tuition and did not like what they found.

To study the issue, PGCC's institutional research office initiated a study of the support offered by Maryland counties to community colleges. The general finding of comparatively low local aid to PGCC was not a revelation to those involved in the college's budget development process, but the size of the difference and its historical consistency was enlightening—and, as it turned out, empowering. In the end, the data produced by institutional research defused a difficult political situation, and an initiative concerning the low level of county support became a routine fixture in the college's strategic plan.

The recession in the early 1990s produced a severe fiscal crisis in Maryland. State revenue shortfalls, combined with mandated Medicaid and welfare expenditures, led to large cuts in state appropriations to higher education and to local jurisdictions. Compounding the problem, community colleges lacked an advocate in the state capitol. The governor had previously announced that the State Board for Community Colleges would be abolished on June 30, 1992. Though a state agency, the board had been an advocate in the capitol for the community colleges. With its demise announced, the board lost its effectiveness—and most of its staff, with employees leaving as soon as alternative jobs were found.

In addition to the financial pressure, other factors contributed to a delicate political situation for PGCC. Prince George's rapidly changing demographics made race a component of many local political issues, and the community college was not immune. In 1988, a state legislator threatened to hold up $1.2 million in state aid to the college pending his subcommittee's review of the college's affirmative action efforts. Later that spring, the college was asked to testify about its minority procurement policy at a county council hearing. A 1991 law changing the state funding formula for community colleges included an amendment requiring PGCC—and only PGCC—to provide a detailed cost analysis report annually to the Maryland General Assembly. Asked why the college was singled out, a state senator replied that in his opinion the college did not adequately reflect or serve the county's 50 percent African American population. Commenting on the tuition increase voted by the board of trustees in response to state aid cuts, the president of the college's Union of Black Scholars stated: "We are taking this personally because this is a direct hit at our people. If they are not in school, they will be in the streets." Several of these issues were played out on the front page of the local newspaper.

During 1991, all of these dissatisfactions coalesced around one issue: PGCC tuition. It had been the highest among Maryland's sixteen locally governed community colleges; the announced tuition and required fees for fiscal year 1992 were 12 percent higher than those of the next most expensive institution. As one state senator asked, "Prince George's Community College is $20 more per credit hour than the community college in the next county. Why?"

Though not always the highest, PGCC's student charges were historically above the average of all Maryland community colleges. Cognizant that the college's tuition was relatively high, the board of trustees nonetheless passed each increase either unanimously or with only one or two dissenting votes. As a group, the trustees were convinced that the college was operating in a cost-efficient manner and that the increases were needed to maintain the scope of programming and quality of instruction they expected of the college.

In January 1991, PGCC's director of institutional research initiated a study of comparative county aid to community colleges in Maryland. The aid that Prince George's County gave to PGCC would be compared to in-state, suburban community colleges of similar size. This ensured that the peer group would not differ in governance structure, state funding, or another fundamental way. Only official, public data sources would be used. Aid would be calculated in three obvious ways: as a percentage of county expenditures, as a percentage of college revenues, and in terms of aid per FTE student. Ten years of data would be analyzed. The final report would display computations as well as trends and include complete appendices of the compiled data. The intent was to present an unassailable product.

The study's design, work, and dissemination were influenced by internal as well as external politics. It was hoped the study would enlighten college employees, if not reduce their anxiety, about the budget and political attacks on the college. Historically, participation in governmental relations and county budget negotiations at PGCC was restricted to the president, his executive assistant, and the vice president for finance. Institutional research had some supporting involvement, conducting environmental scanning for strategic planning and enrollment projections for budget development, but internal strategy meetings were closely guarded. Finally, given that the research office was aware that securing adequate funding for the college was a presidential and board responsibility, findings demonstrating consistently low funding in comparison to neighboring jurisdictions had to be handled with particular care.

The findings were consistent and unequivocal. For ten years, Prince George's County had extended substantially less aid to PGCC than did peer counties to their colleges. This was true across all three methods of analysis. Peer counties contributed twice as large a share of their county budget to support their colleges. On average, the aid contributed by peer counties accounted for 10 percentage points more of their colleges' revenues. Peer counties furnished an average of $700 more per FTE student.

Relating the county contributions to the tuition and fees charged by each college made the relationship clear. Prince George's had the highest tuition because it had the lowest local aid. This finding was buttressed by a companion study of overall college expenditures per FTE, which documented PGCC's relative cost effectiveness. The college was delivering instruction for less money per student than its peers did. Its tuition was the highest to offset the low level of local aid.

Armed with the facts, the research office faced the question of appropriate dissemination. The analysis was first shared in a confidential written report to the president in early February 1991. At the president's request, it was shared with the president's cabinet the next day. The following week, the findings were shared with the board of trustees in a closed dinner meeting; the board then asked that the same presentation be made at the public meeting that followed. In addition, the board asked that a similar analysis of state funding be conducted. Compared to county aid and student charges, state aid was found to be relatively similar across colleges and fairly stable over time. Difference in county aid explained much more of the variation in budget and tuition level than state aid differences.

Following its disclosure at the open board meeting, the analysis was shared with several campus offices at the request of administrators who wanted their employees to gain a better understanding of the county's support for the college. By the end of February, the findings were well known on campus. However, dissemination off campus was not authorized, reflecting the sensitive nature of ongoing budget discussions, continuing uncertainty about state funding, and concern that the information might be perceived as confrontational.

The first off-campus release of the information was mention of the existence of the analysis in reply to a state senator complaining about the college's tuition. No data were shared, only the central finding that the county's support was historically low compared to that of its neighboring peers. Although some administrators argued for full publication of the data in the college's major public relations print piece, which is aimed at county and state policy makers (the college's strategic plan), the president decided against doing so. Instead, he authorized one sentence under the document's planning assumptions: "Prince George's County will continue to provide a lower level of community college support than nearby peer jurisdictions."

The law requiring the college to make a special cost analysis report to the state legislature constituted a rationale for full public release of the county aid analysis. Using this legislative attack on the college to its advantage, the college included the entire study in the report submitted to the state at the end of August 1991. Once this decision was made, the board of trustees asked for a meeting with the county executive so the complete information could be presented to him in person. In September, the director of institutional research made a formal presentation to the county executive and his staff in the executive's conference room in the county office building. The tone was informational, not confrontational, and set in the context of the state reporting requirement. After this meeting, the college decided to share the findings widely. Three tables of comparative data were included in the 1992 edition of the college's strategic plan. Ten years later, the first initiative in the college's strategic plan for 2002 read, "Bolster the county's investment in Prince George's Community College by initiating a program that will increase county funding from 22 percent to 33 percent of the college's operating budget over the next four years."

Dissemination of the comparative county funding analysis succeeded in defusing the high tuition charge. Most criticism shifted away from the college toward the historically low level of county support. Legislators, students, and the public came to understand that variation in student charges reflected differences in county support. County budget staff privately acknowledged that a planned cut in the county's contribution to the college was averted because of the persuasive case made by the college that the county had consistently underfunded it in the past. The data compiled by institutional research prompted addition of a new initiative that became a recurring and prominent part of the college's strategic plan.

What can be learned from this institutional research success story?

- First, *stay attuned to the external and internal decision-making environments.* Know the decisions top management faces and the context in which these decisions will be made. Pay attention to campus politics and relations with external stakeholders. Be alert for opportunities, realizing that timing is crucial to success.

• Second, *take initiative.* Identify opportunities where analysis might be especially pertinent and influential, and go forward. While being sensitive to protocol and personalities, pursue research to completion and put findings in the minds of the appropriate people.

• Third, *be comprehensive in scope but simple in presentation.* Use techniques appropriate to the task. Presentations that are easy for policy makers to understand are preferred; simpler generally is better. Be comprehensive in scope to address all foreseeable alternative interpretations. Preclude anyone in the audience saying, "If you'd analyzed it this way, I bet you would have found a different result."

• Fourth, *turn reporting burdens to your advantage.* External reporting is usually the least rewarding part of the institutional researcher's job. However, as the leverage afforded by the required cost report in this case study demonstrated, occasionally a compliance exercise can become a positive experience for your institution.

• Fifth, *be courteous and respectful when presenting potentially confrontational findings.* Your goal is mutual understanding, not scoring points in a debate.

Conclusion

Institutional research has an established role in the planning process: providing data to support it. Forecasting enrollments and facility needs, conducting environmental scans and internal audits, assessing institutional effectiveness, and assisting in budget development are the explicit, intended contributions of institutional research.

This chapter has argued that ad hoc studies undertaken for purposes other than planning support also can be extremely valuable to institutional planning. It is hoped that the cases presented can serve as a model to inspire similar success stories elsewhere.

References

Boughan, K., and Clagett, C. "A Student Outcomes Typology for Community Colleges: Identifying Achievers with Longitudinal Cohort Analysis." Paper presented at the Twenty-Second Annual Conference of the North East Association for Institutional Research, Burlington, Vt., October, 1995.

Campus Retention Committee. "Campus Retention Committee Final Report, June 1996." Largo, Md.: Prince George's Community College, 1996.

Clagett, C. "Money Matters: Fiscal Crisis as Catalyst to Reform." *Journal of Applied Research in the Community College,* 1994, *1*(2), 101–112.

Clagett, C. "An Outcomes Typology for Community Colleges." *Assessment Update,* 1995, *7*(4), 10–11.

Clagett, C. "Correlates of Success in the Community College: Using Research to Inform Campus Retention Efforts." *Journal of Applied Research in the Community College,* 1996, *4*(1), 49–68.

Garcia z, R. "The Long and Winding Road to the Associate's Degree: Stories Transcripts Tell." *Journal of Applied Research in the Community College,* 1994, *1*(2), 153–166.

Keeton, M., Engleberg, I., and Clagett, C. "Improving Minority Student Success: Crossing Boundaries and Making Connections Between Theory, Research, and Academic Planning." Paper presented at the Thirty-Third Conference of the Society for College and University Planning, Vancouver, B.C., Canada, July 1998.

Pascarella, E., Smart, J., and Ethington, C. "Long-Term Persistence of Two-Year College Students." *Research in Higher Education,* 1986, *24*(1), 47–71.

Seppanen, L. "A Shoe That Fits: A Methodology for Tracking Student Progress in Community Colleges." Paper presented at the Thirty-Fifth Annual Forum of the Association for Institutional Research, Boston, May 1995.

Terenzini, P., Rendon, L., Upcraft, M., Millar, S., Allison, K., Gregg, P., and Jalomo, R. "The Transition to College: Diverse Students, Diverse Stories." *Research in Higher Education,* 1994, *35*(1), 57–73.

Webb, M. "A Theoretical Model of Community College Student Degree Persistence." *Community College Review,* 1989, *16*(4), 42–49.

CRAIG A. CLAGETT *is vice president for planning, marketing, and assessment at Carroll Community College in Westminster, Maryland.*

5

External and internal forces are driving institutions not only to create departments and positions that specialize in planning, quality improvement, and institutional research but also to link them within a systems context.

Linking Planning, Quality Improvement, and Institutional Research

Daniel Seymour, John M. Kelley, John Jasinski

If the reader suspects that this is another pietistic plea for integration and synthesis—for obliterating silos, stovepipes, sandboxes, and other similes of segregation—the reader is right on. The authors believe that overt efforts to link planning, quality improvement, and institutional research can lead to systematic performance enhancement in higher education.

An Argument for Systems Thinking

Appeals for boundary-spanning systems thinking can be traced to Ludwig von Bertalanffy's historic first lecture about general systems theory, in 1949. In that groundbreaking address, von Bertalanffy, generally acknowledged as the father of general systems theory, argued that, as a methodology, systems theory is valid for all sciences. With its emphasis on concomitant perception of the whole and the interdependence of the parts, systems theory has since then become embedded across disciplines. In the field of organizational theory, it has drawn praise especially because its ideas enable observers to see the big picture better. The word *systems* descends from the Greek verb *sunistanai*, which originally meant "to cause to stand together." Systems thinking, in turn, is a discipline for seeing wholes. Gareth Morgan writes that system theory "has helped us to recognize how everything depends on everything else"; it allows "us to break free of the bureaucratic thinking, and to organize in a way that meets the requirements of the environment" (1986, p. 48). In *The Fifth Discipline*, Peter Senge perceives "systems thinking" as a framework and a set of tools, developed over the past fifty years, to make full patterns clearer and to change them. It counters Western reductionism and our tendency "to focus on snapshots of isolated parts of the system" (1990, p 5).

At its broadest level, systems thinking encompasses a large and unwieldy corpus of methods, tools, and principles, all oriented to gaining an understanding of how related elements interact with one another. During the last fifty years, these tools have been applied to a range of corporate, urban, economic, political, psychosocial, ecological, and physiological systems.

Nevertheless, many agree that despite its strengths systems thinking is conspicuously absent in most organizations (DiBella and Nevis, 1998; Senge, 1990). In its place, reductionist imagery, popularized by Sir Isaac Newton and others in the 1600s and extended in the twentieth century by Frederick Winslow Taylor and interpreters (or perhaps misinterpreters) of Max Weber, appears dominant in organizations. Margaret Wheatley, in her widely read book *Leadership and the New Science: Learning About Organization from an Orderly Universe* (1992), sees the majority of today's organizations characterized by a machine model built on the assumption that the system, or the whole, can be understood through knowledge of its working parts. In this model, responsibilities are subdivided into functions; workers are assigned task sets, and page after page of organizational charts serve as blueprints for the workings of the machine.

Geary Rummler and Alan Brache echo this theme in their classic *Improving Performance: Managing the White Space on the Organization Chart*. They discuss a vertical or functional view of organizations, wherein "goals are established for each function independently. Meetings between functions are limited to activity reports" (1995, p. 6).

Unfortunately, organizational participants tend to reduce, think, and describe in terms of hard edges and nice, neat, little boxes. Functional job analysis, for example, helps create job descriptions for the people in the boxes, followed by lines that detail accepted communication patterns. Flowcharting adds other shapes to the boxes; it chunks processes into tidy and tightly linked chains. All of this is further codified through formal policies and standardized operating procedures.

The problem that this chapter addresses is not, strictly speaking, the proclivity to reduce phenomena to composite parts. Reductionism, deconstructionism, chunking—whatever we term it—can be extremely beneficial to understanding, insight, and efficacy. The problem is that this tendency can also push processes, procedures, policies, objectives, and goals toward homeostasis. Even mission and value can undergo an organizational hardening and quickly become obdurate, losing flex and context.

Systems Thinking in Higher Education

Despite the *gravitas* that accrediting bodies and other prominent stakeholders have placed on interdisciplinary learning, systems thinking in higher education is frequently honored in the breach, not the observance.

Nevertheless, marvelous advances have been made in instructional areas such as learning communities, critical thinking skills, and boundary-spanning study opportunities. Reflective practice has touched much of academe. Lecture as the only tool of pedagogy is giving way to a much richer and more respected spectrum of teaching techniques, ranging from technology-assisted instruction to teams, to case-based and problem-based curricula, and to students' planned revision of their written products. Assessment of outcomes has arrived with a flare, transcending levels from specific course outcomes to institutional ones, from the cognitive to the attitudinal. Collaboration between the academic and cocurricular sides of the house is increasing, and there are signs at the administrative level that awareness of new forms of constructive managerial practice is on the rise.

Nonetheless, the culture of the academy continues to revere specialization and boundary building (Cotter, 1998). We too often draw adamant distinctions among student, administrative, and academic functions. Within the academic domain, we have disciplines and departments offering upper- and lower-division coursework. Organizational knowledge tends to be held within a domain; consider how often knowledge transfer still occurs in an isolated classroom setting, with one teacher serving up a lecture in bite-sized portions to twenty to forty students, seated in rows.

Henry Mintzberg (1983) extended this line of thinking in his classic description of the "professional bureaucracy": a highly decentralized organization in which the professionals have considerable control—indeed, autonomy—over their own work, often laboring independently from their colleagues. Citing the university as one of the prototypical professional bureaucracies, Mintzberg observes that supervision is resisted and perceived as an infringement of the highly specialized work of the professor, which demands an equally high level of discretion.

Massy, Wilger, and Colbeck (1994) spotlighted the issue of faculty isolation and fragmentation with their research into the conditions within departments that inhibit faculty members' working together. The two major causes are autonomy ("Overwhelmingly, our respondents identified a central reality in academic life: faculty work alone" [p. 14]) and specialization ("As one faculty member noted, specialization is the route to publication which, in turn, determines tenure, promotion, and salary increases" [p. 16]).

In addition, the relationship between the academic and cocurricular sides of the academy has historically suffered from insufficient respect, distrust, misunderstanding, and lack of shared values, which further dices and divides organizational knowledge (Kuh and Banta, 2000). Traditionally in higher education, we have embraced what Collins (2001) terms level one leadership, in which highly capable but highly partitioned specialists lead the way.

The resulting "hollowed collegiality" is a lack of connectedness, a fundamental fragmentation at the operating core of the academy. Academe has long rebuffed any innovation that has its roots in the business world, but the modern college or university looks more bureaucratic than many modern corporations do. A twenty-first-century corporation is loaded with cross-functional teams and boundary-spanning improvement methods that purposefully work to break down the barriers among the traditional functions of R&D, manufacturing, sales, distribution, and so on (Bok, 2003).

Only recently has higher education examined how we can more effectively manage organizational knowledge, collect and transfer faculty and staff insight, and identify and share best practices from within and beyond the halls of academe. Certainly internal needs and urgencies, perhaps informed by increasingly advanced organizational assessment tools, have spurred this activity. In addition, legislative inquiry, trustee questioning, and accreditation all have nudged institutions to think about (and perhaps act in) a morphed manner.

Planning, Improvement, and Institutional Research

Although most people in this area concur that systems thinking is indeed conceptually broadening, the most oft-heard disparagement over the years is that systems theory is just not specific enough. Khandwalla noted that "What it [the systems approach] fails to do is to spell out the precise relationship" among factors (1977, p. 235). One way to sidestep this is to use case examples and to ground theory in particular experience, as the lead author of this chapter has done in drawing lessons for improving quality and productivity in higher education (Seymour, 1995).

The next chapter in this volume also uses a case study specifically to exemplify the interrelationships among planning, quality improvement, and institutional research. But at this point, it is worth presenting a descriptive baseline for each of the three functions.

The terms *planning, quality improvement,* and *institutional research* conjure up multiple meanings that differ with one's vantage point. For example, a college president may view these functions through an executive, administrative lens while faculty use a collegial, participatory lens. As we consider other stakeholders (students, parents, trustees, legislators), the nuances multiply. For this chapter, the authors choose the institutional perspective but hasten to recognize that this too encompasses diverse frames of reference, such as two-year and four-year institutions, public and private, liberal arts and research, faith-based and secular, single and multiple campuses.

Planning. Dozens of planning paradigms have been advanced, and organizations vary appreciably in how they conduct strategic planning (Hunger and Wheelen, 2003). However, examining planning paradigms reveals common elements among them, and many experts agree with this statement by Pierce and Robinson: "Because of the similarity among the general models, it is possible to develop an eclectic model representative of the foremost thought in the strategic management area" (2000, p. 11). The elements of such a generic, meta-model will hardly startle the reader since they include such familiar terms as mission; values; internal and external environment analysis; identification of strengths, weaknesses, opportunities, and threats (SWOT); strategy formulation; strategy implementation (policies, programs, budgets, programs); evaluation, control, and feedback; and reassessment and improvement. Plainly put, in this chapter we assume that when IR professionals use the term *planning* they basically are talking about a systematic, strategic, action-oriented, institutional-level planning process.

The authors recognize that a host of questions hover around the use of plans and how they function within institutions. Are they stand-alone documents for descriptive show, or are they a force for driving institutional action? How do institutions become plan-driven? How do accreditation and planning relate? Do plans guide resource allocation, or vice versa? Are plans the province of a person, an office, a committee, a community? How do plans cascade to other organizational levels? These are worthwhile and legitimate topics, addressed throughout this volume of *New Directions for Institutional Research.*

Quality Improvement. Ideologically, it seems untenable to argue against institutional improvement, be it continuous or breakthrough in nature. The crux of the issue lies in *how* an organization conceptualizes and operationalizes improvement. Taking a stand-alone pledge of allegiance to quality is insufficient certification that high quality is actually being achieved.

Crisply defining *quality improvement* is elusive. The aliases for quality programs are plentiful. The synonymic swarm can be downright baffling, with handles such as total quality management, continuous quality improvement, performance improvement, quality performance, total quality control, and total quality leadership. In fact, it may be more useful to begin by employing an approach to reasoning that the scholastic philosophers dubbed the *via negativa*—by sharing a few thoughts on what the concept of quality improvement does *not* entail. Quality improvement is not a singular focus on a guru. It is not a simple formula. It is not modular in nature or focused simply on using a set of tools. It is not impersonal. It is not a quick fix. Conversely, quality improvement *is* a mind-set, a way of thinking, a way of being, a way of acting and doing.

For the authors of this chapter, it was heartening to revisit the quality literature and rediscover how often discussion of quality is grounded in philosophy and values. Lewis and Smith, in their popular text *Total Quality in Higher Education,* state that "first and foremost, total quality is a set of philosophies" (1994, p. 29). Cortada and Woods (1995) define "continuous improvement" as "an important value statement." The lead author of this chapter, in his well-known work *On Q,* repeatedly refers to the "philosophy and tools" of strategic quality management (Seymour, 1992). These dual concepts—philosophy and tools—subsequently became requisite design parameters for many successful quality programs. In enduring quality programs, mission and values such as community, service, and stewardship often drive the quality program's commitment to continuously improve all processes and activities through application of a common set of tools and techniques. These tools and techniques are litanized in the quality field: evidence-based decisions using social science and managerial tools, quantitative and qualitative analysis, brainstorming and nominal group techniques, benchmarking, process mapping, flowcharting, Pareto charts, and others. (Many of these tools and techniques are described in some length elsewhere in this volume.)

The organizational shapes that quality improvement takes vary dramatically. At some campuses (for example, Oregon State, Villanova, and Wisconsin), hundreds of personnel and scores of teams have been actively involved in formal quality efforts over the last decade. On other campuses (including Dartmouth and SUNY Binghamton), structured mechanisms and participation are more modest. The critical variable is neither numbers nor structure, but institutionalization of quality—the doing of quality, the culture of quality, quality as a *modus operandi*. In the end, execution is the variable. The differentiator is how the concepts of quality are realized, and how an institution develops and makes real a culture of quality.

Institutional Research. If quality programs labor under an excessive and potentially confusing number of titles (TQM, CQI, TQL, and so on), institutional research (IR) is in the opposite situation. To the authors' knowledge, the expression is used nowhere outside of higher education. The term apparently originated in the 1950s, but the function is hardly recent. The U.S. Office of Higher Education began collecting statistics on higher education in 1869, and by the 1920s units for IR had been established at several major universities (Saupe and Montgomery, 1970). IR is now an academic household word. The Association for Institutional Research (AIR), a national professional group with more than thirty-one hundred institutional researchers, planners, and decision makers from higher education institutions around the world, sees IR as research that improves the understanding, planning, and operation of higher education institutions.

Definitions of institutional research abound (see Terenzini, 1999). One that we like is Dressel's broad description, which casts IR very much like program evaluation: "Institutional research involves the collection of data or the making of studies useful or necessary in (a) understanding and interpreting the institution; (b) making intelligent decisions about current operations or plans for the future; (c) improving the efficiency and effectiveness of the institution" (cited in Saupe and Montgomery, 1970).

However, the singularity of the term *institutional research* is counterbalanced by striking variation in its practice. Delaney's research (2001) reported considerable IR divergence on many variables: function, staffing configurations, locus on the organizational chart, and the academic credentials and experience of IR staff. Some institutions treat IR solely as a reporting function connected predominantly to accountability; others use

IR to formulate and drive their plans. Many colleges and universities have a formal IR office, but it is not uncommon to see these tasks piggybacked onto other administrative or faculty responsibilities.

Linking Planning, Quality Improvement, and Institutional Research

It is clear that more and more institutions are striving to make fact-based or evidence-based decisions. Accrediting bodies, legislatures, and the economy are pushing this, but so are a new wave of administrators skilled in assessment with a vocabulary that does not stutter over applications such as TQM, dashboard indicators, balanced scorecards, and scenario analysis. These and other forces are driving institutions not only to create departments and positions that specialize in planning, quality improvement, and institutional research but also to link them within a systems context. The argument for a systems approach goes well beyond use of data for accountability. Instead, it implies emphasis on converting data to information, information that can steer both strategy and continuous improvement. Effective planning continuously relies on information generated by institutional research, while the principles of quality are powerful in creating a culture of excellence and specific targets for major (and minor) enhancement.

Several chapters in this volume present concrete, case-study examples of effective planning grounded in systems thinking. In particular, the next chapter highlights the functional relationships of planning, quality improvement, and institutional research at a specific institution, Los Angeles City College. Later chapters examine cases where the planning function amounts to a platform for integrating many institutional research and decision-support activities.

References

Bok, D. *Universities in the Marketplace.* Princeton, N.J.: Princeton University Press, 2003.

Collins, J. *Good to Great.* New York: HarperCollins, 2001.

Cortada, J., and Woods, J. *McGraw-Hill Encyclopedia of Quality Terms and Concepts.* New York: McGraw-Hill, 1995.

Cotter, M. "Using Systems Thinking to Improve Education." *About Campus,* Jan.–Feb. 1998, pp. 9–14.

Delaney, A. "Institutional Researchers' Perceptions of Effectiveness." *Research in Higher Education,* 2001, 42(2), 197–210.

DiBella, A., and Nevis, E. *How Organizations Learn.* San Francisco: Jossey-Bass, 1998.

Hunger, J. D., and Wheelen, T. L. *Essentials of Strategic Management* (3rd ed.). Upper Saddle River, N.J.: Prentice Hall, 2003.

Khandwalla, P. *The Designs of Organizations.* Orlando: Harcourt Brace, 1977.

Kuh, G. D., and Banta, T. W. "Faculty-Student Affairs Collaboration on Assessment: Lessons from the Field." *About Campus,* 2000, 4(6), 4–11.

Lewis, R., and Smith, D. *Total Quality in Higher Education.* Delray Beach, Fla.: St. Lucie Press, 1994.

Massy, W., Wilger, A., and Colbeck, C. "Overcoming Hollowed Collegiality." *Change*, 1994, 26(4), 11–20.

Mintzberg, H. *Structure in Fives: Designing Effective Organizations*. Upper Saddle River, N.J.: Prentice Hall, 1983.

Morgan, G. *Images of Organization*. Thousand Oaks, Calif.: Sage, 1986.

Pierce, J., and Robinson, R. *Formulation, Implementation, and Control of Competitive Strategy*. Boston: Irwin McGraw-Hill, 2000.

Rummler, G. A., and Brache, A. P. *Improving Performance: Managing the White Space on the Organization Chart*. San Francisco: Jossey-Bass, 1995.

Saupe, J., and Montgomery, J. "The Nature and Role of Institutional Research—Memo to a College or University." Tallahassee, Fla: Association for Institutional Research, 1970.

Senge, P. M. *The Fifth Discipline*. New York: Doubleday, 1990.

Seymour, D. *On Q: Causing Quality in Higher Education*. New York: Macmillan, 1992.

Seymour, D. *Once upon a Campus: Lessons for Improving Quality and Productivity in Higher Education*. Washington, D.C.: American Council on Education, 1995.

Terenzini, P. T. "On the Nature of Institutional Research and the Knowledge and Skills It Requires." In J. F. Volkwein (ed.), *What Is Institutional Research All About? A Critical and Comprehensive Assessment of the Profession*. New Directions for Institutional Research, no. 104. San Francisco: Jossey-Bass, 1999.

Wheatley, M. J. *Leadership and the New Science: Learning About Organization from an Orderly Universe*. San Francisco: Berrett-Koehler, 1992.

DANIEL SEYMOUR *is provost, Antioch University Santa Barbara.*

JOHN M. KELLEY *is executive director of the Office of Planning, Training, and Institutional Research at Villanova University.*

JOHN JASINSKI *is the principal of Jasinski Consulting Services in Maryville, Missouri.*

PART TWO

Examples from the Field

Stung by a negative accreditation review, Los Angeles City College established an administrative position and a planning process that is successfully creating a culture of continuous improvement. At the core of this success is a "plan-act-check" reinforcing systems loop that links planning, budgeting, and institutional research.

Linking Planning, Quality Improvement and IR: Los Angeles City College

Daniel Seymour

Chapter Five of this volume reviewed general systems theory and how those ideas could conceptually link strategic planning, quality improvement, and institutional research. In the book *Once upon a Campus*, I similarly advocated a systems view as one of the key enablers to enhancement and described efforts at such schools as Jackson Community College, the University of Tampa, and George Mason University (Seymour, 1995). Grounded in firsthand knowledge, a case description of Los Angeles City College is employed here to show how planning, quality, and institutional research have been linked.

Los Angeles City College: The New Ellis Island

Under the watchful eye of the Griffith Observatory and the iconic HOLLY-WOOD sign, Los Angeles City College is the new Ellis Island. There are fifty-five languages spoken within its student body, and only 40 percent of students say their primary language is English. City College is ranked thirty-fifth in the nation for the number of degrees conferred to minorities (*Community College Week*, 2004). The average age of students is thirty. Students' educational goals are both vocational and transfer-related. The college is all about hope and a second chance, and to deliver on this City College awards degrees in sixty disciplines and offers certificates in more than fifty areas.

A Need for Systemic Planning and Management

In 1997 the college went through a difficult accreditation review. The Western Association of Schools and Colleges issued three decisive recommendations. One dealt with the physical environment; the other two, which are directly relevant to this chapter, are enumerated here:

- The institution is severely hampered by a fragmented organization in which planning, research to support that planning, and program review cannot be accomplished effectively. The college needs to improve its planning process, reform its organizational structure, and resolve resource allocation issues.
- The issues of leadership, governance, and district relations are interwoven. College planning is disconnected from district planning and resource allocation, and district goals do not guide the college planning process. The team observed that management and constituency groups operate somewhat independently of each other, and the formal organizational structure does not clearly define lines of authority. To address this issue, college leaders need to accept responsibility for establishing an environment of cooperation and collective ownership of all college issues. The district, as well, needs to recognize and accept its responsibility for establishing an environment conducive to college success.

The language is revealing: "fragmented," "disconnected," "independently." It describes an institution broken into pieces with little sense of the whole or community. This nonsystemic behavior resulted in an organization that was unable to move strategically or share significant experiences. The parts went every which way.

The first step taken to address these issues was structural in nature. The president of the college created a new position for her senior staff team. In addition to the traditional vice presidents for administration, student services, and academic affairs, she developed an institutional advancement function, headed by an executive dean. The responsibilities of this dean were marketing and communications, strategic planning, institutional research, and grants. In retrospect, this initial step was critical. These functions are often slotted into one or more of an institution's silos or are buried deep in the organization structure with little influence. The new office brought glue to the organization.

Some colleges and universities can be characterized as reductionist machine models built on the Newtonian assumption that a whole organization can be understood through knowledge of its working parts. The president of that type of college or university would be the only person with a responsibility to view and manage the organization as a whole. Unfortunately, an individual president's ability to carry out such responsibility is often diluted by a focus on external affairs. As public relations and fundraising continue to dominate a large portion of a president's daily calendar, there is less and less time to embrace the operational aspects of the system. For City College, having a second person with a cross-functional set of responsibilities and perspectives was intended to improve the odds of overcoming institutional fragmentation.

City College's Master Planning Process

A useful way to think about an organizational system is that it can operate through two types of feedback loop: balancing and reinforcing.

A balancing loop generates its own forces of resistance, which eventually bring stability and limit change. These self-regulating systems are seen throughout nature and organizations. For example, the human organism's ability to regulate body temperature is a simple example of dynamic equilibrium—a balancing loop. A reinforcing loop, by contrast, builds on itself. A simple example would be compound interest; the money that is generated builds on itself and can create ever-increasing wealth over time. A reinforcing loop can also spiral downward in a vicious cycle of decline. The point is that reinforcing loops are not about the status quo; they involve change. For an organization, they can lead to cycles of improvement that propel it forward.

Los Angeles City College used the notion of reinforcing loops to develop a comprehensive, integrated system of improvement. As shown in Figure 6.1, the college's master planning process can be described as two linked loops. (The diagram is affectionately known on campus as the "snowman.")

The top loop is strategic and revolves once every six years, moving clockwise. The bottom loop is operational and revolves on a one-to-two-year basis, moving counterclockwise. This creates a reinforcing loop in which any change is magnified over time. In addition, each loop has three components: *plan, act,* and *check.*

Mission and Vision

Mission and vision statements answer the questions, "Why do we exist?" and "What are we trying to create?" A compelling shared vision is at the very heart of strategic planning and continuous improvement.

The process that City College followed began with a visioning team. The team was drawn from several key stakeholder groups—students, faculty and staff members, and administrators, including the president—and its work was facilitated by the executive dean. Members read articles on visioning and reviewed examples of vision statements from a range of organizational types. Several months and a half-dozen meetings later, the team members agreed that they wanted to craft a vision that would accomplish two ends—it would distinguish City College from other institutions, and it

Figure 6.1. Los Angeles City College's Master Planning Process

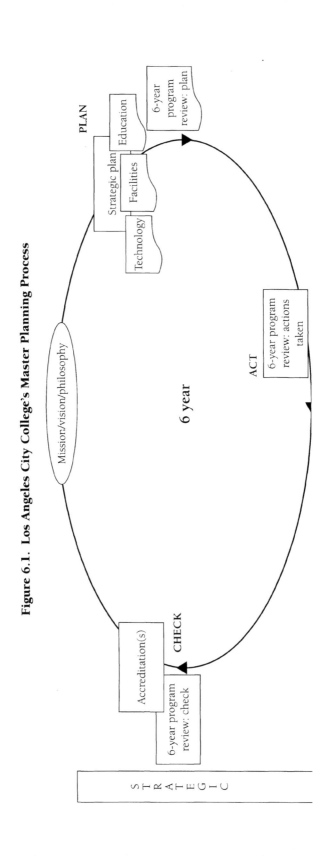

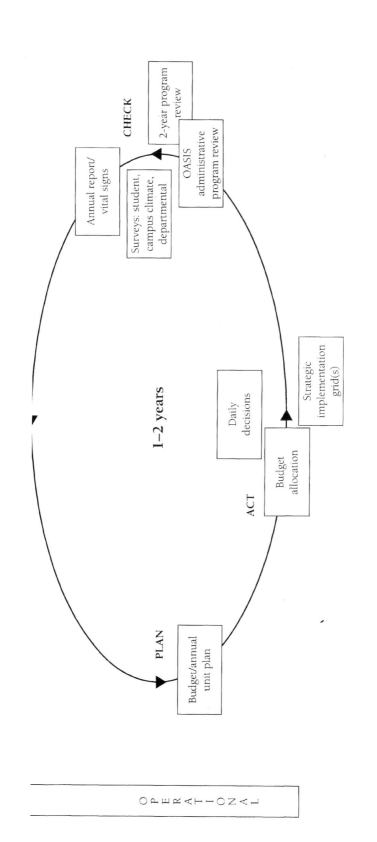

PLAN
Budget/annual unit plan

ACT
Daily decisions
Budget allocation
Strategic implementation grid(s)

1–2 years

CHECK
Annual report/ vital signs
Surveys: student, campus climate, departmental
OASIS administrative program review
2-year program review

OPERATIONAL

would evoke an emotional response—and do it in one sentence! The team delivered. The vision statement, which initiates the reinforcing systems loop, is "Los Angeles City College is an urban oasis of learning that educates minds, opens hearts, and celebrates community." The vision is critical because it empowers everyone in the institution to help create her or his own future.

Strategic Formulation

The strategic planning portion of Figure 6.1 (the snowman) has four documents. The overarching document is the strategic plan, *Creating an Urban Oasis of Learning 2002–2008* (Los Angeles City College, 2002). It was developed over a period of six months in which ten town meetings were held. The town meetings were populated with students, faculty and staff members, administrators, faculty emeriti, and community members; more than one hundred people participated. At each meeting, individuals were asked to reflect on the draft vision statement and the challenges associated with making the vision a reality. To add to this input from the college community, a series of planning assumptions (economic, demographic, educational, public policy, societal, and technological) were generated through secondary research. The resulting plan has eight priorities—for example, to "increase the resources available to the college through state and district allocation processes and through extramural development efforts."

In turn, each priority has an associated set of strategies, such as "Develop and execute a comprehensive resource development plan for the College that includes the Foundation, grants, and business partnerships." In addition, a series of intended outcomes are enumerated, such as "Faculty and staff feel as though they have adequate resources needed to do their work." Finally, there are a series of vital signs, or key performance indicators, such as "number and total amount of annual grants received by the college."

Aligned with the strategic plan are three targeted plans developed either simultaneously with or after the strategic plan. They effectively align with the institutionwide plan. Thus the facilities master plan is aligned with both the vision of "an urban oasis of learning" and priority two: "Maintain and enhance a safe, aesthetically pleasing campus environment that encourages involvement, nurtures community, and leads to student success." A dominant strategic theme throughout the facilities master plan is using landscaping around the perimeter of our forty-eight-acre urban campus to create the feeling of an oasis or safe haven. The educational plan and technology plans are similarly guided by the strategic plan.

The final planning document at the strategic level is the six-year program review. Each academic department is expected to submit materials for approval through the Academic Senate's Educational Planning Committee. The six-year program review (in parallel with regional accreditation) is an intensive analysis that focuses on the strategic direction of a given department. Again, the individual departmental review requires alignment with the educational master plan. Indeed, if the program review document is not completed and accepted by the Educational Planning Committee, the department is not eligible for additional funding.

Working the Plan

The *plan* component of the loop drives the *act* component. As underscored in this volume's introductory chapter by Kelley, Dooris, and Trainer, implementing plans is often neglected; decision makers can forget that the real purpose of planning is not to think but to do. Once a plan is penned, it is essential that someone actually pay attention to implementation.

At City College, the strategic plan is tracked by the Planning Committee of the Shared Governance Council. The council—the representational body that advises the president—has only two committees. The planning committee meets for six months (March through August), and the budgeting committee meets for the other six months (September through February). Chaired by the executive dean, the planning committee's main tool is a Strategic Implementation Grid (see Figure 6.2 for an example). The grid lists each of the thirty-one strategies across the eight priority areas described in *Creating an Urban Oasis of Learning*. It then denotes a "unit of primary responsibility." Because the strategies are frequently cross-functional in nature, task forces are often formed by the planning committee to execute strategies, rather than making assignments to an office or an individual. In addition to identifying the unit with primary implementation responsibility, the grid also delineates a time line for accomplishing goals and has a notes section that allows the committee to capture problems, decisions, and so on.

Evaluation

For City College, the *check* component ("How will we know if we are successful?") at the strategic level involves our regularly scheduled accreditation site visit from the Western Association of Schools and Colleges. As was noted earlier, City College's 1997 accreditation visit sparked the master planning process. However, a six-year accreditation cycle is not appropriate for continuous improvement. Indeed, the scenario associated all too often with accreditation and site visits is a one-or-two-year flurry of activity followed by relative inaction until the next site visit appears on the horizon. Although the planning committee's strategic implementation grid is a useful tool to encourage action to follow planning, there is still a problem. Because planning is not requisite for the day-to-day operations of the college, there is no routine sense of urgency to execute the plan.

This problem is at the very heart of most college planning efforts. For example, it has been an issue both in the area of program review as well as

Figure 6.2. Strategic Implementation Responsibility and Time Frame Matrix

Strategy	Unit of Primary Responsibility	Time Frame					
		2002	2003	2004	2005	2006	2007
Priority 1							
1.1 Develop and implement a new educational master plan that focuses on enhancing the academic enterprise of the core campus.	Subcommittee of Educational Planning Committee	░	░				
An Educational Master Plan was drafted by a subcommittee of EPC. The plan was approved by EPC and the Shared Governance Committee in October 2002.							
1.2 Develop new programs that are responsive to student, industry, and four-year institution needs.	Academic Senate	░	░	░	░	░	░
Six-year program review provides the impetus for this strategy, as does the Educational Master Plan. Implementation of these efforts will occur throughout the strategic planning cycle (*Rev 5.10.02*). In addition, new programs (such as nursing and LAUSD, EPC) should use the Program Viability Process to scrutinize programs and, potentially, revitalize them. As of March 2003, seven programs are under viability (*Rev 4.21.03*).							
Priority 5							
5.1 Research the issue of quality as it relates to student success, and implement a systematic approach to helping students reach their educational goals.	Task Force		░				
Combine with 4.5. Use same task force but gather qualitative data as well. Also links to 1.4. The idea is to develop a critical mass and momentum around specific campus activities. An initial task force chaired by the director of marketing/communications organized "Spring Arts at City" (an insert appears in the *Winter/Spring 2003 Class Schedule*) which coordinates the theatre, music, cinema, and art schedule. The associate dean for community relations has pursued a speakers series that has begun bringing in speakers and the Langston Hughes series; these are examples of campuswide events. Future efforts need to include the Academic Senate (*Rev 11.20.02*). New ongoing programs include the Snyder Lecture, book program, Lombardi series, senate night at the theatre/music/art, and the Gala (*Rev 5.19.03*).							

in institutional accreditation. Indeed, at City College a previous program review process disintegrated because department chairs did not see the relevance to their daily work. Program review became one more tedious add-on that the administration imposed on them. It was a stand-alone exercise. Without the link between planning activities and a tangible benefit to the department, any hope of developing cycles of innovation is improbable.

Continuous Improvement

The purpose of the bottom loop of the Figure 6.1 snowman is to create a linkage such that cause-and-effect relationships are made manifest. If the reinforcing loops are viewed as a pair of gears, the lower gear is much smaller because it turns three to six times as fast as the six-year strategic plan and accreditation cycle.

In the *plan* component, the critical element is building the annual budget. This connecting point between the two loops was created after the college conducted a two-day workshop with staff of the National Center for Higher Education Management Systems. Two take-home lessons from that workshop resonated with the participants:

1. If you don't link planning and budgeting, the budget is your plan.
2. It is never a question of whether the budget is large enough (it never is); it is always a question of whether or not priorities are clearly understood.

The primary tool for bringing these two ideas to life is a standardized Request for Additional Funds, an online form developed by the budgeting committee as a complement to base budgeting. The front of the form asks the department or unit to describe its request and then to give the request a ranked priority. On the reverse side are three questions that pertain to alignment with plans—the strategic plan; the technology, facilities, and education plans; and program review. The answers offered link planning and budgeting; no logical connection, no budget allocation.

Ground-Up Priority Setting

At each level of the organization, priorities are reprioritized. To illustrate, after a department has given priority to its requests the division's academic dean meets with his or her departments. After a thorough discussion, the division distills its priorities. The vice president for academic affairs leads a similar process at the next level up. Finally, at budget committee hearings in January each vice president makes a presentation to pitch priorities and respond to questions from committee members. Each vice president's number-one priority (whether it is personnel, or equipment, or supplies) is placed on a white board and the committee chooses the first priority for the institution. Whatever request is chosen is then replaced on the board by the next request from that area, and the committee chooses again. In this way, the budget committee develops a campuswide list of budget priorities that align with the various plans.

The *act* component follows at the beginning of each new fiscal year. As the vice president of administration and the budget office establish the budget for the year, they are able to advise the committee about how far down the priority list the college can go. Each department or unit's operational budget above its base reflects two things: the size of the budget each year and the relative standing of the unit's priorities compared to other requests. The daily decisions that are subsequently made are investments—that is, allocation of scarce resources to activities that can advance the plans and help fulfill the vision of an "urban oasis of learning."

Data enter the process at several points. As noted, data are used in issue identification, priority setting, and continuous improvement. But nowhere is institutional research more evident than in the final *check* component. Although the vision statement answers the question "What do we want to achieve?" and the priorities and strategies relate to "How will we get there?" the final link in the master planning process answers the question "How will we know if we are successful?" At City College, this is the dominant IR question.

Some portion of the energy devoted by the dean of research and planning goes to obligatory responses to external demands for data, but a stronger focus is inward. The dean's primary responsibility is not on data for accountability but on information for improvement. Working with an institutional research advisory committee, the dean is charged with tracking the metrics that are enumerated in the strategic plan—the vital signs—as well as furnishing departments with information on their key performance indicators (in a two-year program review update).

The real driver of the reinforcing loop is the reporting of the vital signs in the college's annual report. Until recently, Los Angeles City College, like many other colleges and universities, published an annual report that consisted of feel-good highlights. The current document still describes some of the school's major achievements in flowery text, but it also reports on the measures associated with each of the eight priorities. These measures, termed "vital signs," constitute compelling information for improvement; they provide direct feedback on how well the institution is actualizing its vision. As an example, priority six is "Increase the resources available to the college through state and district allocation processes and through extramural development efforts." There are several associated metrics in the 2003 annual report:

- Degree to which faculty, staff, and administrators believe the college is increasing available resources (as reflected by a campus climate survey)
- Number and total amount of annual grants received by the college
- Percentage of the Los Angeles City College District budget that is allocated to Los Angeles City College
- Size of the endowment and number of scholarships awarded

Conclusion

In its second full year of operation, Los Angeles City College's master planning process is working. The Western Association of Schools and Colleges recently completed another site visit, and what were areas of concern on the previous visit have become areas of commendation. The college was praised for its integration efforts: "Previously cited as being 'severely hampered by a fragmented organization in which planning, research to support planning and program review cannot be accomplished effectively,' current efforts to integrate the processes of program review, planning, and budget allocation appear to be effective. . . . Of note as well are the impressive collections of data that are provided by the Dean of Academic Planning and Research and used in evaluation of institutional efforts and for program review" (Western Association of Schools and Colleges, 2003, p. 5).

At the core of this success is a reinforcing systems loop that links planning, budgeting, and institutional research (Figure 6.1). Moreover, as each year goes by and the college makes wise decisions on its resource allocation and executing its plans, it is developing a culture of continuous improvement. The link to performance indicators enables the college to learn and to progress through cycles of innovation. By studying the relationships between things, not just the things themselves, members of the college community are beginning to understand holistically the organization and how it functions. Los Angeles City College, in turn, is creating its own future, as "an urban oasis of learning that educates minds, opens hearts, and celebrates community."

References

Community College Week, analysis of U.S. Department of Education data, Mar. 1, 2004, 12(15).

Los Angeles City College, *Creating an Urban Oasis of Learning, Strategic Plan 2002–2008.*

Los Angeles City College, *Annual Report,* 2003.

Seymour, D. *Once upon a Campus.* Washington, D.C.: American Council on Education/Oryx Press, 1995.

Western Association of Schools and Colleges. "Evaluation Report, Los Angeles City College." Novato, Calif.: Western Association of Schools and Colleges, 2003.

DANIEL SEYMOUR *is provost, Antioch University Santa Barbara.*

7

A new strategic plan, an additional one hundred faculty members, a new financial model, an incentive compensation plan, a new $200 million research building, closing one professional school and repositioning assets to help another, redirecting net revenues from two parking garages, and a building renewal and replacement plan— all are outcomes of a strategic planning and budgeting process.

Strategic Planning and Budgeting to Achieve Core Missions

Heather J. Haberaecker

Northwestern University and its Feinberg School of Medicine adopted a new university and school strategic plan to help the school achieve its strategic vision. This chapter describes how the school organized, planned, and implemented change over a ten-year period, with special attention devoted to the importance of data analysis and to the linkage of the strategic plan to budgeting.

The University and School

Northwestern University is a private, extensive research university consistently ranked among the top twenty research universities in national rankings. With campuses in Evanston and Chicago and a full-time faculty of more than 2,300, the university enrolls more than 13,400 students in ten schools and colleges. Of these, 7,500 students are undergraduates, 2,700 are graduate students, and 3,200 are enrolled in professional schools. The professional schools are the Feinberg School of Medicine, the Kellogg School of Management, and the School of Law, the latter two being recognized as among the best in the country in their respective fields. The university's total operating revenues exceed $1.2 billion, with research expenditures of more than $233 million and climbing.

The Feinberg School of Medicine is located on the Chicago campus. It employs some twelve hundred full-time and sixteen hundred contributed services faculty, educating more than seven hundred medical students and three hundred graduate students, training eleven hundred residents, and conducting basic and clinical research. The school's operating revenues totaled $270

NEW DIRECTIONS FOR INSTITUTIONAL RESEARCH, no. 123, Fall I 2004 © Wiley Periodicals, Inc.

million in FY2002. Research expenditures reached nearly $122 million. Unlike many institutions, Northwestern does not own a medical practice plan or hospital. Rather, with five affiliated hospitals and three major practice plans, all separately incorporated, Feinberg has one of the most complex hospital-practice–medical-school relationships among U.S. medical schools. Therefore, the university and the medical school have far less control over the decisions and assets of affiliated organizations than do most universities that own a hospital or practice plan.

The School's Strategic Plan

Feinberg's strategic plan, published in March 1997, contained this strategic vision statement: "To become one of the nation's preeminent medical schools, as measured by the excellence of our faculty and students, the innovative nature of our research and educational programs, and the quality of clinical care we provide to patients."

To implement this vision statement, the school adopted a series of ambitious plans, including:

- Substantial growth of the medical school by adding more than 100 (later changed to 150) faculty over a ten-year period and building the research, library, and administrative infrastructure needed to accommodate such growth
- Becoming a top twenty research medical center over ten to fifteen years
- Adding more than 250,000 net assignable square feet of research space over the same period, beginning with construction of a $200 million medical research building
- Increasing the breadth and depth of programs in key areas
- Moving from a regional to a national presence in patient care by attracting and retaining top physician faculty and leveraging clinical care with research activity
- Attracting the best (instead of just very good) students and expanding graduate programs in life science to bridge the worlds of research and education
- Reducing the size of the medical school class by 20 percent to better ensure that an outstanding clinical education is provided to all students
- Doubling external support for the medical school in order to finance the plan, with special emphasis on greater affiliate organization and endowment support
- Exploring a new financial relationship with the university
- Committing to regularly budgeting funds to maintain facilities, even if the investment constrains the school's rate of growth

In addition, the plan called for accountability and fiduciary responsibility becoming shared values, and the organization becoming more tolerant of and capable of change by redesigning incentives and expectations to enhance partnering and accountability. Developing indicators and benchmarks to measure the school's success in achieving its plans was also recommended.

Northwestern's Strategic Plan

The school benefited as Northwestern University updated its strategic plan at the same time the school was developing its own plan. This enabled the school to suggest specific strategic directions to university leadership, and to receive definitive responses. For example, when the school was considering how much it needed to expand its research activities and how large its new medical research building should be, university and board leadership both encouraged medical school leadership to increase the size of the building beyond its initial scope and committed resources to this effort. This was in keeping with two of the themes in the university's evolving plan: to grow the research mission on both campuses and to target the Feinberg School of Medicine as an area for expansion and improvement.

In addition, the university's decision to close its dental school allowed a major repositioning of university assets to help support the future of the medical school. The university was able to reallocate shared medical school and dental school endowments and assets (including the net revenue from two parking garages) to the medical school and reallocate dental school space to the medical school to house a portion of the new faculty to be recruited.

Laying the Foundation for the School's Plan

Taken as a single event, development of the school's strategic plan looks fairly similar to that of many strategic planning efforts. For example, the plan was developed through the efforts of a steering committee of which a subset comprised the executive committee, five working groups, an external advisory committee, fourteen topical task forces, and advisory panels (from the five affiliate hospitals, the university itself, and students and alumni). However, it is both the events leading up to development of the plan and those following adoption of the plan that portend much of the success of the plan to date.

For many years prior to adoption of the strategic plan, the executive associate dean for management regularly published and presented comparative and longitudinal data on the medical school compared to other medical schools and to university trends. With the assistance of the director of strategic planning and management, an annual fact book and other analyses were published. They provided longitudinal and comparative data on department and school rankings in research and were based on national norms, trends in funding sources available to the school compared to other medical schools, and trends in university support. Regular presentations on national rankings of departments and other measures were made to the dean's council and departments requesting such presentations. Despite the typical complaints about the quality of comparative data, the school grew comfortable over time with comparative data and understood that data matter. Increasingly, the school understood how data could and should inform the decision-making process.

This openness to data and willingness to embrace the results of environmental scanning helped shape a number of the specific strategic thrusts. For example, the plan to become a top twenty research medical center and recruit more than one hundred additional faculty over ten years was supported by analysis showing how Feinberg's research funding compared to the top twenty research-intensive medical centers as a percentage of overall revenue and what it would require, in the way of faculty and resources, to become a top twenty medical center. Additional analyses showing that the school had a productive but relatively small basic science and clinical research faculty informed the decision to increase the size of the faculty.

Similarly, comparative analysis showed that medical school revenues nationally had increased in absolute terms, but only medical services (practice plan) revenues had increased in relative terms. The results of the environmental scan also showed that medical services revenue was not likely to continue to increase at the current rate because of a medical delivery system that had become more market-oriented. This helped lead to the recommendation to diversify funding sources over time.

A great deal of the success to date in implementing the strategic plan is probably due to its emphasis on a decision-making process informed by data. A number of other factors leading to its success are described here.

Developing and Implementing the Plan

Four factors noted by Anderes (1996) were instrumental in reaching consensus on the school's strategic plan: (1) active leadership from the top, (2) broad participation in developing the plan, (3) regular forums to share information on the plan and its development, and (4) clear intention to link planning outcomes into budget development and allocation.

The university and its board of trustees were active supporters during development of the plan. Much of this was because the individual in the medical school who was leading the strategic planning efforts not only knew planning but could communicate effectively with university leadership and the board of trustees. The executive associate dean for management, who is now the senior executive associate dean and chief operating officer of the medical school, had come from state government and possessed the professional background, relationships, and credibility to deal effectively with the business leaders who served on the board. He also encouraged broad participation in developing the plan within the medical school.

Another factor in the plan's success has been the detailed analyses of the plan's financial viability and development of strategic financial management tools. Detailed financial analyses suggested that the current level of funding would not be enough to support the strategic plan. Therefore, various changes in the school's revenue mix and funding level were modeled, leading to recommended new financial strategies for the school. Development of a new financial relationship with the university and use of some of the revenue to fund a portion of the plan together are one of two key financial strategies emanating from the plan. The other financial strategy—diversification of revenue sources through greater support from affiliate hospitals—resulted from comparative analyses showing that affiliates were contributing substantially less in proportion to the medical school than peer institution affiliates were.

Two other elements had a measurable effect on the success of the plan. The first involved including agreed-on departmental performance indicators in the annual budget and planning process. These measures show each department's performance compared to both the school as a whole and where schoolwide performance ought to be, in such areas as research funding per faculty member and research funding per net assignable square foot of space.

The second factor involved continuously updating the plan on the basis of new information. For example, the recommendation to reduce class size by 20 percent was abandoned when it became apparent that the loss of tuition revenue would only weaken the school's ability to fund the overall plan. Similarly, the number of faculty to be recruited was increased from 100 to 150 when the former dental school space became available, and when the projected costs and revenues associated with each new faculty member were modeled. This is why, as Sevier (2000) says, strategic planning must be a series of conscious, explicit, proactive, and ongoing decisions.

However, changed financial relationships between the university and the school, and between the medical school and its departments, had the most profound effect on the ability to fund the strategic plan.

The New Financial Relationship

The shared strategic vision both parties had for the medical school sparked openness toward changing the financial relationships among the university, the school, and its departments. Nonetheless, the school had to make the formal case for a changed financial relationship with the university and then flesh out the details. School-department relationships under a new financial model also had to be defined before the overall financial change could be implemented.

The Case for Change. As has been noted, financial analyses during the strategic plan's development showed a level of revenue insufficient to fund the strategic plan even when reasonable inflationary increases were included. The university's appropriation to the school, in particular, was growing at a rate of only 3 percent a year, and increases much beyond that rate were not feasible. On the other hand, the school had been experiencing double-digit growth in sponsored research funding since the early 1990s, while gaining only limited sharing of facilities and administrative (F&A) cost recovery revenue. Since both the university and the school wanted to grow the research enterprise, the return of all facilities and administrative revenues to the school seemed logical. Further, the school felt that building incentives into budgetary allocations to departments would further stimulate research growth. The school looked at the various revenue streams the university controlled and was convinced that it should become a "tub on its own bottom"—keeping all of the revenue it earned and paying for the university services it received.

Several other factors led to the decision to forgo an annual appropriation from the university. First, the individual appropriations that some departments received made little sense. Some large departments with significant research and education responsibilities received little appropriation compared with smaller departments with significantly less in the way of research and education responsibilities. These patterns, inconsistent with the new strategic plan, were largely the result of incremental budgeting. Second, the school hoped that by surrendering the appropriation it could demonstrate to the affiliate hospitals and donors that their support would further the research and education mission of the school (rather than subsidizing the university), thus leading to increased contributions. This was important because the hospitals had historically expressed concern that increased support from them could lead to a lower medical school appropriation from the university. Increasing affiliate hospital and donor support was another key financial objective of the strategic plan.

The university agreed to explore options for a decentralized financial management structure for the medical school.

Key Elements of the Change. The university's associate vice president for budget planning and the executive associate dean of the medical school were charged with recommending a decentralized financial management structure that would work for both parties. These two individuals and their staffs reviewed the decentralized financial structures in place at other institutions and visited three of them to learn more about their structures. Ultimately, the team chose to emulate one that had been in place at Vanderbilt University for more than twenty-five years. The Vanderbilt model was selected because the two universities are comparable in both size and mix of programs, including medical schools, and the model was mature enough that most of the issues and problems had been fixed over time. Furthermore, the associate provost at Vanderbilt agreed to provide consultation.

Table 7.1 shows the handling of key revenue and expense streams recommended by the review team to university and medical school leadership. Both parties concurred, with the university adding two refinements. First,

Table 7.1. The Old and New: University-School Financial Relationship

	Historical	Current
Tuition	University keeps	Medical school keeps
Indirects	University keeps	Medical school keeps
Appropriation	University provides	Eliminated
Space, services	University provides	Medical school pays
Earnings on major school endowments and assets	University keeps	Medical school keeps
Capital expenditures	University bears	Medical school bears

it was agreed that neither the medical school nor the university would be disadvantaged financially in the short run (first year), allowing the university sufficient time to transition to the new structure. Second, the university built a president's "tax" into the financial model from the medical school equal to 12.5 percent of facilities and administrative revenue, separate and distinct from the charge the school would be bearing for university services received. The university felt this tax was necessary to give the president sufficient strategic capital to fund university priorities. In part, this was the result of advice received from other decentralized institutions that had failed to build such contributions into their models and subsequently regretted it. Medical school leadership agreed, since the school would be eligible to compete for such funds.

Although both parties relied heavily on data in making their decisions, substantive unknowns still existed at the time the parties agreed to this new financial relationship. First, even though the general methodology of the model had been adopted, no one could predict exactly how much the charge for university services would be, nor the impact on the university of lost endowment earnings now earmarked for the school. Second, neither the school nor the university fully understood the extent of any deferred maintenance obligations the school was assuming. The fact that the change was agreed to, in spite of these unknowns, shows the level of trust that existed between the two parties, and it underscores why trust is viewed as essential to a change of this magnitude (Sanaghan and Napier, 2000).

Decisions Shaping the School-Department Model. The school also needed to determine how to implement a changed financial model internally. The executive associate dean and director of strategic planning and management conducted additional analyses and decided that critical decisions involved:

- How much of the new revenue available to the school would go to departments as opposed to staying at the school level
- Which costs under the new model would stay at the school level instead of going to departments

- Clarifying financial responsibility for strategic growth of the medical school
- Funding the school's educational function
- Funding the medical school's administrative costs

Splitting Revenue, Allocating Costs. Of the three major new sources of revenue (tuition, facilities and administrative revenue, and centrally held school endowments), the first two are generated by departments. It was clear from the outset that a major portion of these revenues should be returned to the departments, to replace the appropriations they previously received from the university and to help create some incentives to support the school's growth. The question then became, "How much of these revenues should be returned to departments?" This question could not be answered until it was decided how to handle the new costs to the school associated with the financial model. These costs included paying the university for medical school space, services received from the university, and the president's tax.

The space question was relatively easy to answer. It was decided to pass space costs on to departments to help influence their decision regarding how much space they really needed. A related decision involved using only one rate for all types and quality of space to simplify the allocation procedures.

However, deciding how to allocate the costs of services received from the university was complicated by the fact that the model for assessing costs to the school had not yet been fully developed; nor had the total cost been determined. The school had to make some assumptions about what the total costs would likely be. The costs were modeled using the school's share of university administrative costs that the latter provided to the school, as reported on the annual financial survey submitted to the medical school accrediting body. The other related decision was whether to pass these costs, as well as the cost of medical school administration and the president's contribution, on to the departments, thus showing full costs at the department level. Use of a full-cost model would have helped the departments understand their real costs, but it was felt that the burden of additional transactions on an outdated university accounting system was not worth the benefits that would be derived. Furthermore, these were not costs that departments could control. Therefore those costs were taken off the top using a tax rate structure before distributing remaining revenues to departments.

Responsibility for Growing the Enterprise. A decision on how to fund the 150 new faculty and related needs called for in the strategic plan was another consideration factored into the internal model chosen. Analyses showed that the clinical departments had substantial revenue available to them from the transfer of practice plan revenue and from endowments provided by grateful patients. It was also clear that the basic science departments did not have similar resources available.

A model was constructed to estimate the average expected costs and revenues for new faculty hires—incorporating start-up costs, ongoing support for a portion of salary, expectations about revenue generation, and the like. This model was based on the school's own experience and survey results of experiences at other medical schools. The analysis showed that most clinical departments could afford to finance the cost of new faculty, but basic science departments and a few clinical departments could not. Therefore it was decided to allocate a portion of new revenue for the strategic growth of the medical school using the tax rate structure already noted.

Funding the Education Function. At Feinberg, basic science departments bear primary responsibility for educating medical students during their first two years. These departments previously received the largest appropriations from the university; they were the only medical school departments with tenure and the financial guarantees associated with it. Because they did not have the same diversity of resources available to them as did the clinical departments, they had the most to lose under the new financial model. On account of the university's financial guarantee to tenure and the lack of other resources, it was decided to fund a portion of each tenure-track faculty member's salary from the tuition dollars now available to the school. However, guaranteed financial support for faculty was ramped down over a three-year period, from 50 to 45 to 40 percent of salary, and then stabilized at that rate to give departments time to grow their research function.

Tuition funds also were distributed to departments to support their education function, with a specific allocation model developed by the executive associate dean for education in collaboration with the school's Education Council. Since there are few national norms in this area, development of the model has proven difficult and thus far has not received widespread support. In its current and most simplistic form, it is designed to accomplish two objectives: (1) allocate funds to departments to support the educational administrative roles they perform using a standardized rate; and (2) allocate funds in proportion to the actual teaching performed by the department, with separate weightings by course type.

Medical student financial aid was historically provided from endowments and a university appropriation to the school. Since the school would no longer receive a financial aid appropriation, the medical school tuition revenue stream was deemed the most appropriate funding source for the portion not funded from endowments.

Funding Medical School Administration. The cost of medical school administration was historically funded from the university appropriation, school endowments, and support from the medical school's practice plan. A new funding mechanism was needed to support the lost appropriation as well as fund additional administrative costs associated with new space and other infrastructure needs. These costs were built into the tax rate structure as well.

The Final School-Department Model. Many analyses were conducted—for example, of the amount departments would receive under

Figure 7.1. Funds Flow Under the New Model: School-Department Relationship

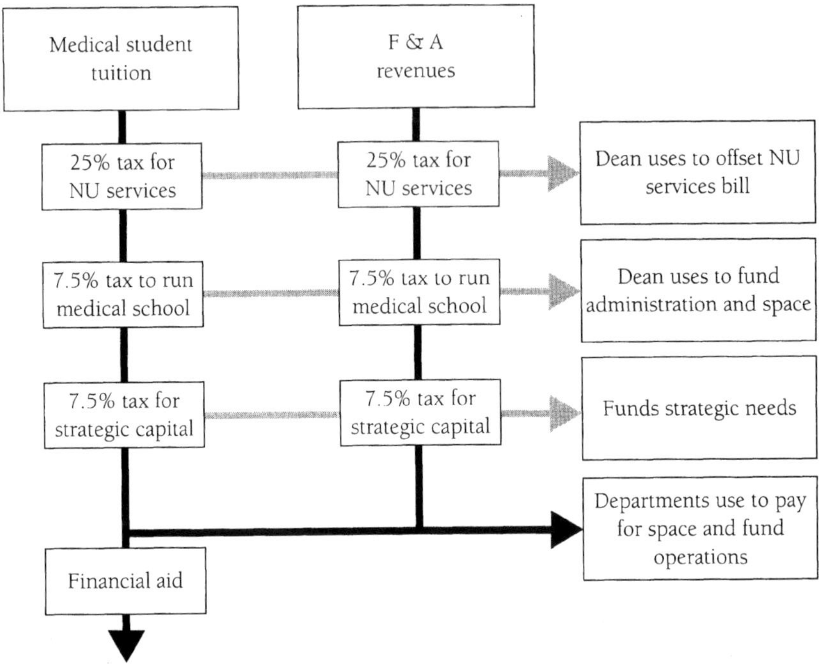

various scenarios compared to previous appropriations, how much would fund medical school administration, and so on—to create the model shown in Figure 7.1. This illustrates how the two primary revenue streams (medical tuition and facilities and administrative revenue) are being taxed. The one cost missing from this model is the required president's tax, which is being funded from the endowments transferred to the school.

As the internal school-department model was developed, several objectives drove specific decisions, among them a desire to:

- Understand the costs (space, services, administration) and their relationship to the tax rate structure
- Create incentives for growth and optimal use of resources at the department level
- Support strategic goals of the school by requiring all departments to participate in funding the strategic capital needed to grow the enterprise
- Move authority, responsibility, and decision making down to the department level on matters such as faculty productivity and space management

- Make the model as rational as possible by having funds flow proportionally to activities that generate them

Implementation Phase. The implementation phase consisted of three components: (1) determining the methodology for the university shared services assessment, (2) deciding when and how to move to the new financial relationship between the university and school, and (3) selecting an implementation strategy within the school.

Shared Services Assessment. Early in the process, the university and school agreed to use revenue rather than expense as the basis for determining the school's proportional share of university services costs. This decision was reached largely by default. The alternative would have involved determining the percentage of effort expended by each administrative office on medical school activities; this was viewed as too cumbersome, too subjective, and probably too unstable to support sound management year to year.

Three major efforts were required to build this model: (1) allocating the various university revenue streams to the proper school, college, or administrative unit; (2) netting noneconomic activity out of university administrative expenses to ensure that shared services expenses were allocated fairly; and (3) determining which revenue streams were the appropriate basis for setting the medical school's share of expenses. Shared services rates developed from the ratio of medical school to university revenues were applied to the applicable university administrative costs to determine the medical school's share of university services costs. Information flowed freely between the two parties during development of the model, and the medical school was a major player in determining which revenue streams were appropriate in determining our share of expenses. Table 7.2 shows the percentage of university services costs that the medical school paid in FY2002.

Pulling the Trigger. When and how to implement the new financial model was the subject of much debate between the university budget and planning office and the leadership of the medical school. The school in particular worried that other university goals and priorities would take precedent over the new model if it were not implemented within a year of agreement having been reached. The budget office, on the other hand, worried that it did not have the necessary infrastructure in place to implement the new model. A compromise was eventually reached whereby the two parties agreed to:

- An overall control number that the medical school was allowed to budget for FY2001, based on a very conservative estimate of facilities and administrative revenue, real likely space costs, and an estimate of the likely university shared services assessment.
- Distribution of only part of the endowment funds and none of the parking garage income that were to come to the school under the new

Table 7.2 Summary of FY2002 Shared Services Assessment Calculation ($ in Thousands)

	NU Total Cost	FSM Share	% of Total
Administration	$15.96	$3.18	19.9%
University services	5.36	1.14	21.3
Business and finance development	17.57	4.81	27.4
University relations	2.87	0.81	28.2
Enrollment	7.73	0.33	4.3
Student affairs	10.93	0.41	3.7
Research administration	8.84	3.54	40.0
Graduate studies	1.99	0.16	8.1
University library	20.75	0.15	0.7
Recreation (Evanston)	3.67	0.00	0.0
Information technology	—	2.04	—
	$104.99	$19.19	18.3%

financial model. The university was bearing the full cost of closing the dental school, and this was part of the strategy to hold the university harmless in the first year of the transition.

• Agreement to make no major changes in the university's accounting system for FY2001 as a result of the change. This required the school to run its own shadow system to ensure that it was earning an amount at least equal to the control number.

• Agreement to fully reconcile revenues and expenses under the model following FY2001. The school would receive any additional revenue earned above the control number but would also be responsible for any shortfalls.

The School's Implementation Plan. The school needed to accomplish two objectives in its implementation of the new financial model: first, develop a strategy to ease in departments that would have fewer resources than when they received direct appropriated funds; and second, develop a budget strategy for FY2001 yielding departmental allocations equal to the agreed-on control number. These objectives were interrelated, but the need to grant the basic science departments a longer transition period was recognized early on, given their heavier reliance on the university appropriation. As has already been noted, the reserved education pool allocation to the basic science departments was structured so that support of faculty salaries would decrease from 50 to 45 to 40 percent over a three-year period. Further, it was decided to hold all departments harmless during the first year (and only the first year) of the new model to give them time to adjust to the new realities.

To finalize the department budget allocations, the school relied on the tax structure developed to allocate revenue streams to departments and used the earned education pool allocations developed by the executive associate dean for education. Two other decisions were required. The first was how to fund the "hold harmless" provision for all departments losing under the model. The second concerned distribution of resources under the control number between departments and the dean's administration. It was decided to fund the hold-harmless provision by reducing the net new revenues available to advantaged departments by 50 percent. Thus new phrases were coined: "stop-loss" and "stop-gain" provisions. It was decided to furnish the remaining funds to the dean's administration even though it represented a loss for FY2001 compared to the previous appropriation. This was viewed as acceptable, since it helped build departmental acceptance of the new model. The dean's administration also had other resources available to temporarily offset the loss. Also, beginning in FY2002, the school would be receiving additional endowment income and proceeds from the parking garages that had been withheld in FY2001.

Implementation Problems Experienced. The problems experienced are grouped here under three broad categories: (1) technical, (2) conflicting roles and responsibilities, and (3) communication.

Technical. Regarding technical problems, the university lacked the fund and account structure to transition easily to the new financial model. The school's need to see the revenue earned against budget in real time challenged the university's conventional ways of doing business, and it required difficult changes in the university's outdated accounting system. Even with these changes, it was hard to manage the day-to-day operations of the school's finances, since the system required a larger number of accounting transactions and redundant shadow fund information. The lack of a muscular reporting tool or data warehouse at the university level further compounded the problems; some of the deficiencies of the university's transactional accounting system could have been overcome by having more readily available and flexible reports.

Another major problem has been integrating data from the student information system and the financial accounting system to give the school the necessary input on tuition earned and financial aid costs by program and student. Nowhere has this problem been more pronounced than in the graduate programs. Although much progress has been made in this area, more still needs to be done.

Conflicting Roles and Responsibilities. With the exception of the associate provost from Vanderbilt who helped build the model for calculating the university's shared services assessment, all of the work involved in moving to the new financial model fell on individuals with ongoing roles and responsibilities. This is significant because Northwestern has always prided itself on having a lean administrative staffing structure. Many individuals find it difficult to devote time to the analytically complex issues that must be addressed in developing and implementing the new model, while keeping daily operations functioning smoothly.

Time constraints also led to a delay in finalizing agreements about the shared services assessment and other model components. These problems were not insurmountable, but it is essential that such ground rules be written so that they are explicit and understood when, for example, the players change.

Communication. Although the vice presidents and deans of other university administrative units were informed of the change in the financial relationship between the university and the medical school, it is not clear that they fully understood the implications for their areas. Perhaps the essential aspects of the change were not reinforced frequently enough to become transparent. It is clear that the heads of other areas have not fully understood how the shared services assessment model works; as a result the associate vice president for budget and planning had to intervene.

Similarly, the school has had some internal communication challenges. As noted earlier, the school's model for distributing earned education pool funds to departments has not been well received. This is due in large part to using two models and four major weighting changes in three years, resulting in large fluctuations in department budgets. However, there has also been insufficient communication and understanding of the earned education pool model. For FY2004, there has been a pronounced improvement in communication with departments regarding the model. This has gone a long way in reducing the noise level. But some problems are likely to remain until there is a more stable model.

One of the tenets of the new financial model is to openly share information about the financial status of the enterprise, but because of time constraints this has not occurred as soon or frequently as desired. Thus departments have engaged in debate over resources that might have been minimized had more information been shared.

Capital Planning

Under the new financial model, the school has complete financial responsibility for building, renewing or replacing, and maintaining its physical assets. A key component of the strategic plan involved building a new $200 million medical research facility to accommodate many of the 150 new faculty to be hired under the plan. With a $40 million lead gift, this building is now under construction and is expected to be 100 percent funded from philanthropy, as is all new construction at the university. It is not practical to present details about the capital plan here, but capital planning has been integrated and concurrent with the strategic planning and budgeting initiatives described in this chapter.

Linking Strategic Planning and Budgeting

Since the late 1990s, medical school departments had been doing all fund budgeting, whereby the revenues and expenses of all entities supporting the departments were reported, including those of the practice plan and affiliated hospitals.

Medical school administration took this all-funds-budgeting approach further by developing a more comprehensive set of multiyear financial projections that encompassed, for example, revenue and costs of strategic actions, the new debt service required under the capital plan, revenue and expense associated with renewal and replacement, and depreciation (explained later). The revenues and expenses associated with the 150 new faculty positions were calculated using the model described previously, with projections shown through FY2011, the year the school will be at steady state—with new faculty generating the expected level of grant as well as facilities and administrative revenue.

The projection model is flexible enough to determine whether the revenue available is sufficient to fund the nonrecurring and recurring costs of new basic science faculty, and whether the clinical departments are able to fund their share of new faculty. It is also possible to adjust the mix of faculty as well as other assumptions in the model, to estimate their projected impact.

Higher education institutions do not typically record depreciation expense for buildings and capitalized equipment on their balance sheets; it was important for the medical school do so since it is totally responsible for funding its own capital plan. Furthermore, the affiliate hospitals from which the school sought continuing contributions do include such costs on their balance sheets.

An analysis is currently being completed of unrestricted fund balances across the medical school, including expendable endowments. This information should enable school administrators to know the level of contingency funds available to fund unexpected needs or meet unanticipated shortfalls.

The development of a financial projection model covering both operating and capital needs has done what Jones (1995) suggests a good strategic budgeting process should do: give university leaders a tool for ensuring the long-term adequacy and integrity of institutional assets. The model and resulting bottom line have been instrumental in gaining university support for debt financing of $50 million for the capital plan. They have also been important in seeking additional ongoing and unencumbered support for research and education from the affiliate hospitals. As noted previously, the affiliate hospitals extend less support on average than do hospitals at counterpart institutions. Their support would do much to wipe out the negative bottom line that the model is currently projecting.

The new financial model and financial projection model have been powerful incentives and tools. The financial model explicitly sets aside budgeted funds for priorities established in the strategic plan. Using a multiyear financial projection model expands horizons and allows the school's leadership to determine which components of the strategic plan are doable, and when, and with what tradeoffs. Departments are now in control of their own destiny and can increase their staffing and budget according to their own effort. This constitutes the direct tie-in of unit budgets and activities advocated by Knepp (1992).

What Are the Outcomes of Strategic Planning?

George Keller (1999–2000) has suggested that strategic planning is increasingly about organizational learning and creativity, and that there is a need to change radically existing structures and processes. The Feinberg School of Medicine has seen evidence of "organizational learning" since its new financial model was implemented:

- Grant activity and facilities and administrative revenue are up, with F&A revenue 18.5 percent higher in the first year of the change and 15 percent higher in the current year.
- Adoption of an incentive compensation plan for basic science faculty in FY2002 helped increase the percentage of faculty salaries on grants in basic science departments, lessening the burden on departmental budgets.
- Department chairs are making tough decisions, such as returning unproductive space and encouraging early retirements.
- Departments are becoming more selective in their faculty hiring decisions, looking at prospective faculty members' likely research output and how well they fit with the priority areas of the strategic plan.
- It has been easier to recruit department chairs under the new financial model.
- Departments are increasingly using their own resources for faculty recruitment, and in some cases sharing the cost of recruitment packages with innovative payback mechanisms.

The school is at a critical phase of implementing its strategic plan. The medical research building comes online early in 2005, and another large amount of space will be put in service in 2004. The school has recruited thirty-three net new faculty of the 150 targeted. Recruitment needs to ramp up substantially to fill the new space. Fundraising for the new building has slowed down substantially, owing to the downturn in the stock market and continued fallout from September 11, 2001. Negotiations are at a critical stage with our affiliate hospitals regarding a continuing, unencumbered contribution.

There are always challenges such as these to be overcome. The medical school can adapt, using the skills shown during development of the strategic plan and the change to the new financial model:

- Embracing the results of environmental scanning
- Continually updating the plan and assumptions on the basis of new information

- Taking a multiyear approach to implementation of the plan
- Taking advantage of opportunities when they present themselves, and always remaining flexible
- Continuing to furnish incentives to achieve the objectives of the strategic plan

Recent results of an environment scan are leading the school to question the planned mix and number (150) of new faculty, with the thought that recruiting fewer faculty at higher ranks may be an effective alternative. Ideas such as this will be debated across the enterprise. One notion that is likely not to be debated, however, is that data matter.

References

Anderes, T. K. "Connecting Academic Plans to Budgeting: Key Conditions for Success." In B. P. Nedwek (ed.), *Doing Academic Planning: Effective Tools for Decision Making.* Ann Arbor, Mich.: Society for College and University Planning, 1996.

Jones, D. P. "Strategic Budgeting: The Boards Role in Public Colleges and University." (AGB Occasional Paper Series, paper no. 28.) Washington, D.C.: Association of Governing Boards of Universities and Colleges, 1995.

Keller, G. "The Emerging Third Stage in Higher Education Planning." *Planning for Higher Education,* 1999–2000, 28(2), 1–7.

Knepp, M. G. "Renewal in the 1990s: The University of Michigan Initiatives." In C. S. Hollins (ed.), *Containing Costs and Improving Productivity in Higher Education.* New Directions for Institutional Research, no. 75. San Francisco: Jossey-Bass, 1992.

Sanaghan, P., and Napier, R. "Deep Lessons About Change in Higher Education." *Business Officer,* 2000, 34(4), 32–36.

Sevier, R. A. *Strategic Planning in Higher Education: Theory and Practice.* Washington, D.C.: Council for Advancement and Support of Education, 2000.

HEATHER J. HABERAECKER *is associate dean for finance and budget/chief financial officer in the Feinberg School of Medicine at Northwestern University.*

8

Integrated planning promotes collaborative thinking and furnishes mechanisms for linking strategic plans with operational plans.

Integrated Planning for Enrollment, Facilities, Budget, and Staffing: Penn State University

Louise E. Sandmeyer, Michael J. Dooris, Robert W. Barlock

Penn State, a multicampus land grant university with locations throughout the Commonwealth of Pennsylvania, has used a universitywide, ongoing, annual strategic planning process since 1983. Beginning with a pilot program in 1999 and continuing through the present, the university has incorporated integrated planning into the planning and improvement process for eighteen of its twenty-four campuses. This chapter describes Penn State's experience in launching that effort, and it highlights lessons learned.

What Is Integrated Planning?

The term *integrated planning* is encountered in a variety of settings, such as transportation, land and water use, architectural engineering, energy, manufacturing, the military, and state and local government. Not surprisingly, the elements that factor into integrated planning vary with the domain. For example, integrated planning for religious ministries is designed to help churches simultaneously evaluate issues such as the desirable size and growth of their congregations; management of finances, fundraising, and debt; pastoral and support staffing; and build-versus-renovate decisions (Living Stones Associates, 2004). The specifics would differ for a manufacturing firm or municipal government, but in principle the impetus for integrated planning is consistent: namely, to explicitly relate strategic organizational decisions that affect one another but that might otherwise be dealt with through separate processes.

NEW DIRECTIONS FOR INSTITUTIONAL RESEARCH, no. 123, Fall 2004 © Wiley Periodicals, Inc.

The concept of integrated planning is emerging in higher education. The 2003 conference program for the Society for College and University Planning listed it as the theme of four sessions. The National Association of College and University Business Officers has begun offering a continuing professional education course entitled "Integrated Planning and Budgeting" (NACUBO, 2004). Integrated planning is becoming an explicit part of some university strategic plans (Atkinson, 2002; University of Alberta, 2004), and several chapters in this volume touch on the subject.

In higher education, integrated planning draws together such activities as strategic planning, capital and operating budgeting, enrollment management, and human resource planning, which might otherwise be somewhat disconnected. Integrated planning usually means enhancing collaboration of operating units—academic schools and colleges—with support functions such as the budget office and physical plant. In addition, it may push planning across multiple levels of the institution, spanning central university and unit-specific decision making. Typically, integrated planning also extends over a multiyear time frame, of about three to five years. Atkinson describes the rationale for integrated planning this way: "There is the promise of integration in integrated planning. With multiple revenue sources, multiple capital demands, and a changing student and faculty demographic, it is no longer desirable (if it ever was) to make one-off decisions or lavish attention on a selective subset of problems. We have to raise our decisions to a higher level" (2002, p. 6).

The Penn State Scenario

Penn State overlaid integrated planning onto its existing strategic planning and improvement processes in 1999, two years after reorganizing its campus college system. Eighteen of Penn State's twenty-four campuses historically served mostly as two-year feeders to the central campus. In 1997, this system was reorganized to alleviate enrollment pressures at the main University Park campus by encouraging the campuses to offer carefully selected four-year degrees. An enrollment-driven budget model was put in place, making available to the campuses the resources and incentives to develop offerings that met market needs in their respective geographic areas. Suddenly, Penn State's campus colleges were dealing with a new set of unfamiliar and significant planning challenges.

In 1997 and 1998, campuses struggled to meet these challenges. In the interest of increasing their enrollment (and corresponding share of tuition revenue), campuses began creating programs and admitting students that the existing infrastructure could not necessarily support. They rented trailers for temporary classrooms and scrambled for off-campus housing. There were concerns about whether the pool of faculty was sufficient to deliver new academic programs, and about how increased demands for cocurricular programs could be met. Admission decisions made at some campuses intensified the already stiff competition for upper-division slots at the central campus. Ironically, this was one of the concerns that led to the campus college reorganization in 1997. In short, the university needed a more systematic and integrated approach.

Development and Implementation

In 1999, Penn State's provost and the senior vice president for business jointly charged a team with developing an integrated planning model for the university's campus colleges. The executive director of the Office of Planning and Institutional Assessment chaired the eight-person team, whose members included administrators from key areas (budget, enrollment management, finance and business, physical plant) as well as selected data stewards.

The first task the team undertook was to compare the macro schedules and timing of key events across four distinct planning cycles (academic, capital, budgeting, and enrollment) to improve alignment, reduce redundancy, and streamline processes. The team then distilled key measures and indicators for enrollment, staffing, capital funding, facilities operating costs, and anticipated revenues and expenditure, thus formalizing the interrelationships among these management processes.

The Planning Schedules

To assist the campus colleges in data collection, the team created schedules (worksheets) for the processes to be integrated. For example, the office of enrollment management developed an *enrollment schedule,* the budget office developed a schedule to address *staffing,* and the office of physical plant developed a schedule for *facilities.* In all, seven schedules were developed. Each included baseline data, plus open cells in which to project data for the next five years. These were the seven schedules:

1. *Admission and enrollment,* for enrollment projections
2. *Staffing requirements,* for faculty, staff, administrators, technical service workers, and other positions to support changes in enrollment and programs
3. *Capital plan,* for assignable square footage already in the facilities inventory or else funded and scheduled for occupancy within the current five-year capital plan, by the type of space (classroom, lab, office)
4. *Capital projects,* to document land acquisition, new facilities, and major renovations, with capacity indicators (such as number of beds and parking spaces)
5. *Capital funding plan,* to identify sources of funding for all capital projects
6. *Tuition income, salary expenses, and departmental allotment and wages,* presenting total projected revenue from increased student enrollment, as well as the costs associated with added staffing

7. *Increased new facilities operating cost,* presenting the additional costs associated with new or newly remodeled facilities

The schedule in Figure 8.1 is a sample worksheet from the 2002–2005 planning cycle.

The Process

Integrated planning was conducted as a pilot program for the eighteen selected locations in 1999. Since then, it has been on an alternate-year schedule. Integrated planning complements the annual, ongoing strategic planning and improvement processes in which campus colleges (as is true of all Penn State units) continue to participate.

Enrollment is the driver for integrated planning at Penn State, and the first schedule that campus colleges must complete is a preliminary enrollment plan. The campus colleges work with the office of enrollment management to project enrollments realistically. It is important for campuses to forecast *total* enrollment, not just freshmen admissions, to assess whether existing or planned human and physical resources will accommodate total campus enrollment.

Preliminary enrollment plans are due in September and include projection five years out. The enrollment schedules are reviewed by the university's Central Enrollment Management Group, the provost, and the president. After receiving relevant feedback on their enrollment plans, campus colleges receive the remaining schedule templates with instructions. These are completed and submitted by February 1 (which is also the due date for strategic plans) to the Office of Planning and Institutional Assessment, which coordinates the data management process.

The Office of Planning and Institutional Assessment merges the schedules from individual campuses into a unified database, facilitating cross-campus comparison. The package can easily be transmitted electronically among various offices and campus colleges.

Figure 8.1 footnote   →

Note: *Upper division enrollment: the total number of baccalaureate degree candidates with a semester classification of 05 and higher. There are four mutually exclusive subtotals provided.

Your college: the number of students at this campus enrolled in a major authorized by your academic college.

On behalf of another college: the number of students at this campus enrolled in a major of another college, where the program is designated to be offered at this campus (for example, IST).

Approved exceptions: the number of students at this campus enrolled in a major of another college, where the student has been given special permission to enroll at this campus (example: a junior who has been given permission to remain for one additional year).

Remaining common year/DUS—The number of students at this campus who have yet to enter a degree-granting major.

Figure 8.1. Schedule 1: Admissions and Enrollment Planning

Schedule 1: Campus/College Admissions and Enrollment Planning

Enrollment Planning	Base	Projections				
	Fall 2000	Fall 2001	Fall 2002	Fall 2003	Fall 2004	Fall 2005
New first-year students						
Baccalaureate (freshman admits)						
Associate						
Provisional						
Graduate						
New advanced-standing students:						
Baccalaureate						
Associate						
Continuing students:						
Baccalaureate						
Associate						
Provisional						
Graduate						
Nondegree students						
Total campus enrollment	0	0	0	0	0	0
Full-time equivalent (FTE)						
FTE/total campus enrollment (ratio)						

Admissions Planning

Freshman baccalaureate admissions target (Su/Fa)						
Actual/estimate paid accep'ts (Su/Fa)						

Change Of Assignment

Target change of assignment to UP						
Actual/estimate (Fa/Sp) change of assignment to UP						
Change of assignment to other Penn State campuses (except UP)						
Change of assignment from UP to your campus						
Change of assignment from all other campuses (except UP) to your campus						

Enrollment Indicators

Upper division enrollment*						
Your college						
On behalf of another college						
Approved exceptions						
Remaining common year/DUS						

Campus baccalaureate graduates (fall/spring/summer)						
Campus associate graduates (fall/spring/summer)						

First Evaluation

After the initial pilot in 1999, an evaluation of the integrated planning process was conducted and improvements were made. The most significant change was to better synchronize the integrated planning process with submission of units' three-year strategic plans or annual updates to the provost, so that campus colleges would be given feedback in time to revise and resubmit their integrated plans with strategic plan updates. This timetable offered an opportunity to further use the schedules as a planning tool, and to better ground the units' strategic plans.

Second Evaluation

A second, more thorough evaluation of the integrated planning process occurred in June 2003. This evaluation included all of the participating campus colleges. Open-ended questions were posed around five themes:

1. Adequate communication of the purpose and expectations of the process
2. Clarity of instructions
3. Quality of support received from four central offices (of planning and institutional assessment, physical plant, enrollment management, and budget)
4. Benefits of participating in the process
5. Suggestions for improvement

More than sixty individuals who had taken part in the integrated planning process were invited to participate in the evaluation. Respondents included data stewards and campus executive officers. The response rate was almost 70 percent for campus executive officers and just over 50 percent overall.

Respondents generally felt that the integrated planning process enhanced decision making. They also offered specific suggestions for improving the process.

Suggestions for Improvement

Many of the respondents' suggestions were specific to Penn State, addressing, for example, the lack of a quality-of-space indicator in the facilities inventory database (this example and others are not detailed here).

What may be more interesting (although not surprising) to institutional researchers elsewhere is that many of the challenges involved data definitions and discrepancies. The integrated planning process showed that not all campuses were using the same working definitions and conventions, even for measures that are frequently used (for example, the calculation for an FTE faculty member or FTE student). Because data are collected in different ways and at different times of year, some comparisons were difficult, and there was disagreement about numbers. For example, tennis courts had been converted to an overflow parking lot at one campus, but this change had not yet reached the central data files. More important, discrepancies in classroom square footage were common and often resulted in recount and remeasurement of facilities. Further, the comfort level and data acumen were uneven among those responsible for completing the schedules. This variation resulted in considerable rework and consultation for those in central offices supporting the project. In any case, the next iteration of the integrated planning process, beginning in fall 2004, will surely benefit from improvements in these areas.

Benefits

As described earlier, Penn State adopted integrated planning in response to a concrete, specific problem. The university's leaders saw a need to better manage enrollment growth and its effects at campus colleges, and the process seems to have helped in that respect. Objective data (for example, on admissions, enrollments, and enrollment flows) suggest that the difficulties leading to integrated planning have been ameliorated.

Subjectively, participants recognize significant benefits as well. For example, an individual campus college projecting vigorous enrollment growth but only a modest increase in staffing can now easily see the net effect on student-to-faculty ratios. Campus colleges can quickly gauge financial implications of an academic plan, as well as identify the time frame during which additional faculty, staff, and facilities are likely to be needed. The package also enables quick comparison of variables (such as student-to-faculty ratio) across campus colleges, highlights current and projected trends and outliers, and enhances the central university-level planning perspective.

Campus executives have noted that integrated planning promotes critical and collaborative thinking, and that it reinforces the university's expectation that strategic planning will be firmly rooted in data. Here are representative comments received from campus executive officers and staff:

"Integrated planning helped us with long-term planning and with broad comparisons with other academic units for benchmarking purposes."

"It caused us to look at how we were using space and led to some new efficiencies."

"This process provided me an opportunity to interact with our campus enrollment officer and share ideas and concerns on future enrollment."

"I made extensive use of the report and data as part of our strategic planning process, and most recently in our campus efforts to initiate our ten-year master plan."

Conclusion

Penn State has had long-standing strategic planning and continuous quality improvement programs. The more recent integrated planning process is succeeding for several reasons; one may be that it is perceived as a pragmatic complement to strategic planning and as a tool for improvement, fitting Penn State's culture.

Integrated planning has been a mechanism for linking strategic plans with operational plans, and it has served as a vehicle for testing assumptions and projecting scenarios. Integrated planning has helped foster direct analysis of the impact that enrollment has on other critical components such as staffing and space. The package gives Penn State campus colleges a chance to review and validate their measures with the offices of physical plant, budget, and enrollment management.

Penn State's integrated planning is highly enrollment-dependent and builds on an enrollment-driven budget model. Admittedly, projections are imperfect. Nonetheless, the process has helped to clarify what were once only implicit assumptions. Integrated planning has also helped decision makers revisit their projections and make needed adjustments and refinements.

Cross-campus comparative data have been useful not only to the units but to central administration as well. Participants note that the process has fostered collaboration and communication within each campus, and between the campus and the central university offices responsible for enrollment, staffing, facilities, budget, and strategic planning.

Finally, periodic evaluation contributes important benefits. Evaluation helped shape the program during its first four years, and it continues to suggest improvements.

References

Atkinson, M. "University of Saskatchewan: The Provost's White Paper on Integrated Planning." Saskatoon, Saskatchewan, Can.: University of Saskatchewan, 2002.

Living Stones Associates. "Integrated Planning Track," 2004 (http://www.living-stones.com, retrieved Apr. 22, 2004).

National Association of College and University Business Officers (NACUBO). "Integrating Planning and Budgeting," 2004 (http://www.nacubo.org, retrieved Apr. 21, 2004).

University of Alberta. "2002–2006 Strategic Business Plan: Update 2004." Edmonton, Alberta, Can.: University of Alberta, 2004.

LOUISE E. SANDMEYER is executive director, Office of Planning and Institutional Improvement, Penn State University.

MICHAEL J. DOORIS is director of planning research and assessment at Penn State University, in the Office of Planning and Institutional Assessment.

ROBERT W. BARLOCK is a planning research and assessment specialist in the Office of Planning and Institutional Improvement at Penn State University.

*Over the past decade, cross-functional quality
improvement teams have been formed not only to
reengineer work processes but also to enhance community
and create incentives and recognition; they have moved
the university from planning to action.*

A Team Approach to Goal Attainment:
Villanova University

John M. Kelley, James F. Trainer

Planning at Villanova University takes place on a variety of levels. The
board of trustees and president impart general direction to the university
and approve all new academic programs. The Administrative Planning and
Budget Committee (APBC) serves as the institution's preeminent internal
planning body. Each college (and many academic and administrative units)
actively engages in strategic planning processes. The governance structure
as well as Villanova's approach to accreditation and its quality initiative
create rich opportunities for planning input from faculty and staff. This
case study describes a pair of innovative projects that feature cross-
functional teams.

In February 2001, the board of trustees approved a set of twelve strategic goals for the university, recrafted from a list of fourteen. These goals
describe the critical and enduring qualities that will characterize Villanova
over the next ten years, solidifying its position as a leading Catholic institution of higher education. The goals set a tenor and tone for the university
and help identify whom the university serves, what it will offer, and how it
will operate.

The goals are directed at fulfilling the mission of the university. They
state that Villanova:

- Will be a Catholic university that reflects Augustinian traditions, nurtures
  the development of religious faith and practice, develops the moral and
  ethical perspectives and values of its members, and fosters social responsibility and commitment to service

- Will be a community of men and women increasingly diverse in culture, ethnicity, race, and socioeconomic status and welcoming to individuals of diverse religious traditions
- Will achieve excellence in all undergraduate programs, which will have a strong liberal arts and sciences component, and in the offering of selective graduate and professional programs
- Will attract, retain, and recognize a scholarly and caring faculty who are respectful and supportive of the university's mission, who are committed to distinction in teaching, learning, and research, and who are generous in service
- Will enroll and retain a national and international student body of a progressively higher academic quality
- Will provide an educationally purposeful living and learning environment rich in opportunities for personal, intellectual, social, cultural, artistic, and professional growth
- Will provide and maintain state-of-the-art facilities and technologies appropriate to the academic, personal, and administrative needs of the community
- Will offer equitable athletic opportunities at the intercollegiate, intramural, club sport, and recreational levels, and achieve national recognition in selected programs
- Will govern by principles of collegiality that involve faculty, staff, students, alumnae/i, administrators, and trustees
- Will commit human and financial resources to advance the university's primary goal of education as articulated in the university's mission statement
- Will foster strong relationships with alumnae/i, parents, friends, and the local community
- Will measure the achievement of strategic goals throughout the university and use the results for continuous improvement

A Team Context: The VQI Initiative

As indicated in its mission statement, Villanova's initiative, Villanova Quality Improvement, is an effort to deepen the university's communal bond, sense of shared purpose, and openness to change in order to better serve students, parents, colleagues, alumnae and alumni, and others through striving for continuous improvement in relationships and work processes.

One of the original 1993 core principles of VQI, and one that has endured, is *teamwork*. Over the past decade, hundreds of cross-functional VQI teams have been formed, some devoted to reengineering work processes and others whose purpose is enhancing community and creating incentives and recognition. The two teams described in this case study operate within this context.

Strategic Goal Attainment Teams

Time-tested, highly respected systems for strategic planning typically include, as a core function, strategic goals monitoring. A unique feature of planning at Villanova was the formation, in 2001, of a strategic Goal Attainment Team (GAT) for each of the university's twelve strategic goals. This system of teams replaced a prior process that had largely been limited to gauging performance on a number of indicators with a carefully selected group of comparison institutions.

At Villanova, the primary planning body is the APBC, which consists of five vice presidents, four academic deans, and four directors, among them the executive director of planning and institutional research. An APBC member serves as a direct liaison to each GAT team in order to ensure first-hand communication. This APBC liaison either chairs the team or delegates the chair responsibility to another team member. Team members are recruited from the most appropriate colleagues across the campus; hence the majority of teams are cross-functional. Villanova faculty and staff populate these teams, whose charge is "to concentrate on a specific goal in order to monitor progress, facilitate and suggest strategies for actualizing goals, and in other ways to enhance goal-driven strategic planning." The value added by these teams is their ability to craft finely textured evaluations featuring factors germane to each goal.

During the initial cycle, each team worked throughout the fall 2001 semester and made a formal presentation to the full APBC in December 2001. Two full days were set aside by the APBC for this reporting function, which was characterized by detailed, evidence-based presentations of goal attainment and collegial dialogue regarding accomplishments, challenges, and continuous improvement. Holding these sessions during the fall semester permitted any adjustments requiring budgetary action to be implemented promptly, even as early as the next fiscal year. A second round of GATs is now under way and it is planned that this process will repeat every two to three years.

The Goal Attainment Teams enhance goal-driven strategic planning at Villanova by suggesting specific performance indicators, measuring progress toward goals, and stimulating dialogue for continuous improvement. Thus in reporting to the APBC each team responds to a series of questions:

1. How will we know when Villanova has attained this goal? (That is, is there an appropriate, realistic target for this goal? How is the goal operationally defined?)
2. How far along is Villanova in attaining this goal? (Quantitative indicators are emphasized.)
3. How well is Villanova progressing toward this goal?
4. What would be the three most important steps that the university could take to promote attainment of this goal?

5. Are there other factors that the APBC should take into consideration about this particular goal?

For example, the Office of Planning, Training, and Institutional Research (OPTIR), under the direction of its executive director, serves as the GAT for strategic goal twelve, calling for the university to measure the achievement of strategic goals and to use the results for continuous improvement. To facilitate realization of this goal, after conducting a survey of campus leaders about the use and status of previous strategic plans, reviewing accreditation processes, and examining indicators of success suggested by other GATs the team recommended that the APBC:

- Ask each unit to monitor and update its goals annually and provide this feedback to its supervisor in the form of a written report
- Conduct regular strategic planning workshops to help ensure the continuity of the planning process, especially as units experience change in leadership
- Develop, in a collaborative effort among the APBC, OPTIR, and the various GATs, a core set of twelve essential performance indicators ("dashboard indicators") for the university to track in an effort to monitor the status of the university at the aggregate level

In addition, OPTIR indicated that the university must develop means not only to monitor its success but also to ensure that a feedback loop exists to permit continuous improvement. Asking all units to monitor their goals annually ought to establish a mechanism for effective decentralized planning across the university, while concomitantly monitoring the twelve essential indicators. Thus the APBC maintains its role in overseeing the university's overall strategic progress.

Middle States Self-Study Implementation Team

A second effort in the realm of teams was development of an implementation team to follow through on the recommendations of the accreditation self-study process. This self-study was part of the decennial accreditation by the Middle States Association of Colleges and Schools Commission on Higher Education. The self-study involved almost two hundred Villanovans working in assessment task force teams that generated 159 recommendations, augmented by ten recommendations from the visiting evaluation team. Such recommendations have a habit of sitting on a shelf and coming to life in a dither when accreditation time draws near again. To counter this custom and link the self-study directly to planning, an implementation team was assembled promptly on completion of the accreditation self-study. Team members included key academic and cocurricular administrators. OPTIR was named to lend support and technical assistance.

The implementation team followed a set of specific tasks:

Reviewing and sorting the 10 recommendations from the visiting team and the 159 recommendations from the self-study into two generic categories, "strategic" and "operational"

Dividing the operational recommendations into two sets: (1) those that can be implemented by a single department and (2) those that are cross-functional in nature

Subdividing the cross-functional operational recommendations into those that are primarily academic and those that are primarily cocurricular

Referring strategic recommendations to the APBC, the university's planning body

Referring single department operational recommendations to the appropriate department under whose aegis the recommendation falls

Referring cross-functional operational recommendations that are primarily academic to the vice president for academic affairs

Referring cross-functional recommendations that are primarily cocurricular to the Division of Student Life or the VQI Council as appropriate

Requesting that the appropriate bodies review each recommendation and determine whether it has already been implemented, can be implemented immediately, will be implemented during next academic year, will be implemented if funding request is met, or will be put on hold until a specified date or be rejected

Requesting that each appropriate body report disposition of the recommendation back to the implementation team so that a Central Status File (CSF) is maintained

Periodically reviewing the CSF to determine if updated information is needed for certain recommendations, and contact the appropriate person to obtain the same

Preparing a formal report for the Middle States 2006 Periodic Review Report

The implementation team divided into eight subteams of one to three members each, charged with monitoring various thematic categories of recommendations. For instance, one subteam sought to track the recommendations that dealt with Villanova's institutional integrity and mission, while another tracked the recommendations relative to students and student life, and a third addressed the academic enterprise (faculty, educational program and curricula, library and learning resources, and institutional effectiveness and outcomes). In most cases, these clusters directly reflected topics from specific chapters of the self-study report.

Over the summer of 2002, the subteams gathered information on the status of each recommendation falling into its area. A matrix was produced to classify and monitor the status of the recommendations, with each row containing key information on a given recommendation. The twelve columns each contained a specific piece of information about a given recommendation and the status of that recommendation. The matrix was migrated into a database that allowed sorts and merges in any number of ways. The matrix was made available through the campus intranet. A system was devised whereby those on subteams responsible for tracking the outcome of particular recommendations can insert updates to their status via the Web. The status of all recommendations is updated at least annually.

Table 9.1 presents a description of the columns included in the matrix.

In all cases, recommendations are categorized as (1) having been completed, (2) ongoing, (3) pending, (4) rejected, or (5) remaining unaddressed. Recommendations are considered to be pending if additional decisions or resource allocations are needed before the recommendation can be fully implemented.

At the end of the first review period, approximately eighteen months after the evaluation team's visit, the implementation team reported that ten recommendations had been fully implemented, eighty-six were ongoing, sixty-six were pending, ten remained to be addressed, and only three had been rejected.

Finally, each recommendation was matched with one of the twelve strategic goals of the university. As a result, the recommendations contained in the implementation team matrix can inform planning at Villanova in many ways. For example, they can be employed in the work of the APBC's strategic GATs.

The OPTIR played a key role in the development, successful launch, and continued progress of the implementation team. OPTIR developed the protocols and procedures that drove this process. Specifically, the office:

- Culled the recommendations from the self-study and visiting team reports and sorted them by chapter or task force
- Identified and extracted each of the suggestions from the visiting team's report
- Took the first pass at sorting the recommendations into strategic and operational categories
- Prepared a document for the implementation team containing all of the recommendations and suggestions as sorted
- Facilitated an initial meeting of the implementation team at which point the team was divided into subteams and each subteam was assigned the responsibility for tracking the disposition of recommendations in a given area
- Developed a matrix and populated it with information that facilitated tracking recommendations in a common format across areas

Benefits of the Team Approach

A number of benefits derived from use of teams in monitoring and facilitating strategic goal attainment at Villanova. Specifically, the teams helped to ensure that planning documents remained alive and active and that the

Table 9.1. Information Contained in Implementation Team Recommendation Matrix

Column	Information	Column	Information
1.	Tracking number assigned to each recommendation	7.	Contained a note on current progress on the recommendation
2.	Actual verbatim recommendation	8.	Indicated current status of the recommendation
3.	Identified recommendation as either strategic or operational	9.	Identified whether additional, new funds are required to implement the recommendation and, if so, how much would be needed, if known
4.	Indicated whether Villanova self-study or the visiting team was the source of the recommendation	10.	Listed any notes related to the recommendation and noted if supplementary, explanatory information was available on file
5.	Identified the office(s)/individual(s) most likely to have an interest in the recommendation being implemented	11.	Noted the primary strategic goal of the university to which the recommendation could be tied
6.	Identified the person(s), office(s), or decision-making body with the authority to determine whether a recommendation would be pursued and, if so, to allocate resources toward it, if needed	12.	Noted any additional strategic goal(s) or subsection of strategic goal(s) to which the recommendation could be linked

university took full advantage of planning opportunities. The teams assisted the university's move from planning to action. The teams also helped maximize the utility of work already being produced and helped create synergy between various planning efforts by linking the recommendations of the implementation team with the strategic planning goals. In a sense, this helped bridge top-down (APBC-initiated) and bottom-up (generated by the accreditation self-study) approaches to planning. Moreover, the teams facilitated community engagement and involvement in both the strategic planning process and the follow-through of the Middle States accreditation process. Ultimately, task forces were empowered in that they could see their work being used and making a difference. As a byproduct, the lead role the OPTIR staff played in each of these processes helped raise the visibility of the IR office on campus.

JOHN M. KELLEY *is executive director of the Office of Planning, Training, and Institutional Research at Villanova University.*

JAMES F. TRAINER *is director of planning and assessment at Villanova University.*

A future-search conference is a participatory planning and decision-making process in which a group of individuals with diverse perspectives come together; engage in a process of data collection, discussion, and learning; and decide on an appropriate course of action. The competencies, skills, and intellectual capital developed as part of this search conference had a significant impact on the faculty.

Future-Search Conferences at Cornell University

Chester C. Warzynski

A fundamental challenge in higher education is reaching consensus with faculty and staff on decisions about strategic issues and actions. The strong culture of individualism found in many institutions often militates against coordinated action. Many strategic planning efforts fail to achieve their full potential because they do not build a foundation of common understanding or generate the commitment needed to achieve desired results.

The need to gather information from multiple knowledge domains to guide future direction is critical in academic decision making and planning. A future-search conference[1] can be a vehicle for accomplishing this in a way that satisfies participants and improves individual commitment. A future-search conference is a participatory planning and decision-making process in which a group of individuals with diverse experiences from the same or differing organizations come together; engage in a process of data collection, discussion, and learning; and decide on an appropriate course of action.

The search conference is usually conducted over a period of one to three days, and it may involve from ten to hundreds of participants in a focused and collaborative discussion around issues and challenges facing the organization. A future-search conference is based on the premise that the people most closely associated with the work have valuable information and experience from which good decisions can be made and appropriate actions determined. The participation of these individuals in an open and self-regulated planning and decision-making process leads to greater understanding, which in turn yields greater coordination and commitment, as well as better results.

The search process consists of four major activities: data collection, data analysis, decision making, and action planning. The process begins with a structured inquiry based on several key questions about the organization and its environment. The data generated from this inquiry are aggregated and classified into themes. Then both the implications of the themes themselves and some proposed actions are identified and ranked by the participants. Finally, an action plan is developed to achieve the desired results.

Future-search conferences have been used at Cornell to develop strategic plans for colleges and departments, reorganize and merge departments, respond to external reviews and accreditation reports, and even prepare grant proposals. This case study describes how a future-search conference was used to structure a conversation with a multidisciplinary group of faculty in the Department of Population Medicine and Diagnostic Sciences to build a group understanding of the challenges faced by the department, and to develop a strategic plan in response to an external accreditation review. Although this case describes a single academic department, the methodology of the future-search conference can be engaged effectively at the level of a professional school or university as well.

The Case of Population Medicine and Diagnostic Sciences

Cornell is a world-renowned research university recognized as a leader in a number of academic fields, among them veterinary medicine. The Department of Population Medicine and Diagnostic Sciences is at the forefront in addressing population medicine and public health in veterinary biomedical research. The department has an outstanding diagnostic laboratory; expertise in design and analysis of population-based studies; a network of clinical, outreach, and extension professionals; and a strong connection with animal industries and the state of New York. Its faculty members are recognized leaders in their scientific disciplines and publish extensively in internationally recognized journals.

The mission of the department is to promote health, productivity, and welfare of food- and fiber-producing animals, companion animals, and wildlife populations; ensure safety of foods of animal origin; prevent animal disease; and reduce associated risks to human health.

In May 2002, the chair of the department, Yrjo Grohn, with the assistance of the university's office of organizational development services conducted a one-day future-search conference for faculty. In addition, academic staff members were invited. The conference was conducted with a total of thirty-eight participants, nineteen faculty members, and seventeen academic staff, with the expressed purpose being to develop a strategic plan for the department.

Planning an effective future-search conference involves five steps: (1) creating clear objectives or outcomes for the conference, (2) determining the questions that need to be answered, (3) collecting and processing information and experience, (4) aggregating and categorizing the information and experience, and (5) deciding what action to take to achieve the outcomes.

In terms of the first step, the objectives of the conference described in this case were defined this way:

Create a forum for the faculty of the Department of Population Medicine and Diagnostic Sciences to share information and perspectives on the future of the department

Identify critical competencies and capabilities for achieving and maintaining excellence in research, teaching, and clinical service

Develop a new and innovative vision of what the department can become once those ideas have been realized

Revise the departmental review document and develop a strategic plan including goals, strategies, and actions

Determine what faculty requirements, resources, and communications are necessary to execute the strategic plan

An e-mail survey was distributed to the faculty participants prior to the retreat. The survey contained a series of questions deemed important to the future of the department. The chair conducted the survey (which is optional in a future search) to give the participants more time to think about the questions that would be used in the interview process and to develop more substantial perspectives around the issues facing the department. The findings from the survey were distributed to the faculty, for their information and study, one week prior to the retreat. The faculty were asked to examine the data with an open mind and a view toward learning, as well as to construct their responses for the one-on-one interviews that would take place at the conference. The survey data were retained as contextual information and used in developing the final written plan.

These were the survey and interview questions addressed by the faculty and staff in the future-search conference:

- How do you expect our discipline(s) to change nationally and internationally?
- What are the core areas or areas of expertise in the department?
- What core values should guide our decision making?
- What goals, projects, or initiatives should be pursued over the next five years?
- What criteria should be used in hiring new faculty?
- What specific steps should be taken to improve quality of research and teaching?

A one-day future-search conference usually addresses five to eight separate but related questions; as many as twenty-four questions might be answered in a three-day search conference. The group's answers to these questions are translated into the themes, goals, strategies, and actions that are subsequently included in the strategic plan.

In a future-search conference, chairs are arranged in pairs facing one another, with the number in each row determined by the number of questions to be addressed. In this case, six questions were used, so there were six people in each row facing each other, or a total of twelve individuals participating in the same group. (There can be as many as eight groups of twelve, or even more, participating in a future search.) Each person in each row received one of the six questions for use in conducting her or his interviews. Each person is responsible for conducting a three-to-five-minute interview using the same question with each of the six individuals seated directly across the row. In other words, each person is acting as a reporter interviewing six people, using the same question.

During the data collection step, each participant in the first row begins interviewing the person directly facing. At the end of the first three-minute interview, the interviewer and interviewee switch roles. The person in the second row then interviews the person in the first row for three minutes. After the individuals facing each other have completed a round of interviews, the participants in the second row rotate by moving one seat to the right (the person at the end of this row rotates back to the first chair in the row, and the participants in the first row remain stationary). This process of rotating interviews is repeated until all participants in each row (1) have interviewed all six participants across from them, collecting information on their question, and (2) have been interviewed on all six questions by the participants from across the row.

If the number of individuals in the group is fewer than the total number described here, one or more questions can be removed from the group; or some individuals can be instructed to conduct their interviews using more than one question. If the number of individuals in the group is larger than described here, participants can be instructed to conduct joint interviews. A second option, if the number of participants at the search conference is larger than twice the number of questions used in the interviews, is to form a separate small group of participants to answer all the questions in sequence as part of a small-group brainstorming session. In this case, the data gathered for each question are recorded on a separate sheet of paper and delivered to the subgroups responsible for aggregating and categorizing the data (as described later).

The second step in the future-search process is to have all participants take about ten minutes to organize the information in the notes they took during their interviews by identifying the ideas and themes that are (1) highly representative of their group, (2) somewhat representative, or (3) unique. After each individual has organized his or her information, subgroups are formed of individuals with the same question. In this conference of thirty-six people, there were three groups of twelve people answering six questions. In turn, six question subgroups were formed. The small subgroups aggregate and summarize their information and report their ideas and themes in the three categories to the larger group.

Following the subgroup reports, the larger group engages in a multivoting exercise (in which each person gets five votes to identify key priorities for certain questions and may use up to two votes on any two items as a method of weighting the importance of certain items) to identify the "best" or most significant ideas or themes. Typically, only questions requiring immediate action are voted on (for instance, "What goals, projects, or initiatives should be pursued over the next five years?").

Once the key ideas and themes have been identified and voted on (and are visible to the entire group on chart pads), the facilitator leads a short discussion in which the priorities are summarized and consensus is established. Consensus is defined as "a tentative willingness to accept the results determined by the group, pending further evaluation."

An optional final step in the future-search conference is to create small groups to flesh out the ideas and themes, and to develop action plans (action steps, responsibilities, deadlines, and resource requirements). In the action planning process, the small groups complete an action plan for each major priority or project, specifying key actions, targets dates, responsibilities, and resource requirements. Each small group reports its action plan to the plenary group for questions and ratification.

To summarize, the agenda for a one-day future-search conference includes these steps:

1. Introduction, objectives, and explanation of the logistics of the conference (fifteen minutes). Participants interview each other for three minutes per question. In this example, six questions take thirty-six minutes. Given time to move from chair to chair, this part of the exercise normally takes about forty-five minutes.
2. Participants organize the information by themselves (ten minutes).
3. Break (fifteen minutes).
4. Participants work with other people who have the same question and aggregate and categorize their ideas or themes (sixty minutes).
5. Lunch (sixty minutes)
6. Group presentations: twenty minutes for each group (120 minutes, or two hours).
7. Break: during the break participants engage in a multivoting exercise to identify their priorities for key questions, with the facilitator tallying the results (fifteen minutes).
8. The group engages in an action planning exercise to develop the first cut of project plans (sixty minutes).
9. The facilitator leads a short discussion on participant reactions to the exercise process and results and determines next steps (thirty minutes).

The total time in this process is seven to eight hours.

Outcomes

The future-search conference described in this case created a body of meaningful and useful information for defining the future of the Department of Population and Diagnostic Sciences. The themes, goals, and strategies of the future-search conference clustered around a number of ideas:

- Pathogenesis of infection and disease, and development of appropriate diagnostic tests
- Dynamics of diseases in animal populations, for building science-based health programs
- Education of students, graduates, the public, and animal industries so they can understand the principles underlying diagnosis and dynamics of infection and disease in animal populations
- Design of programs to promote the health and welfare of animals and production of high-quality, safe animal-based foods

The future-search conference generated a vision for the department and created a mandate for action based on clear goals, strategies, and action plans. The faculty and academic staff were pleased by the process and supportive of the results. In general, the group felt that the conference produced a clear direction for the future, better awareness of the critical competencies and capabilities needed to meet future challenges, and an improved sense of confidence in working together as a team to accomplish departmental goals.

Evaluation of the search conference yielded an average rating of 5.62 on a scale with the highest possible rating being a 7.0. No item on the evaluation received a rating lower than 4.0, with most ratings being sixes and sevens. Here are representative comments from participants:

> We achieved more meaningful results than I anticipated in a short time. It was a good and refreshing experience, meeting and working with others in the department, identifying common issues to move the department and the diagnostic lab into the future. There is more in common among colleagues than there are differences.

> It was the best department retreat that I have been involved in. This retreat involved the largest number of department faculty that have come together in the past several years. We must make sure the items actually happen and that we use this information.

> I enjoyed knowing all the different people and interacting with them in an informal setting that allows open conversation. The format allowed everyone to contribute and consolidate diverse ideas. I liked the model followed to reach consensus. It was well organized with good flow and focus. It will go a long way in promoting personal and working interactions.

> It exceeded my expectations for facilitating communication. I enjoyed the efficiency. We were able to accomplish most of our goals. It was generally well organized and processed.

> Enlightening. . . . enjoyed getting together and sharing ideas. The small group discussions enabled us to work out details for implementation of goals.

On the other side, a few participants were uncomfortable that important decisions were made in such a short period of time ("Too much ground covered in too short of time"; "Time limitations associated with issue development"). These observations are legitimate concerns, but the scope of the discussion and time limitations have not prevented the department from achieving significant results, as indicated in the conclusion of the department chair:

> The retreat influenced our actions. We are very heavily involved in zoonotic research [animal diseases that are a risk for human health]. We recently received a $6.6 million grant from the NIH to establish a Zoonotic Research Unit at Cornell. In addition to this grant we have received several other grants in the area of food safety, diagnostic testing (part of a $3 million Johne's disease grant). We are in the final stage of hiring four faculty members (two in clinical pathology, one in endocrinology, and one in clinical toxicology). After these four hires we will start a search for an immuno-geneticist and then a microbiologist. Well, a lot of things have happened because of our retreat."

Conclusion

This case study describes a future-search conference in the Department of Population Medicine and Diagnostic Sciences in the Veterinary College at Cornell University. One of the goals of the future search was to develop a strategic plan for the department and a response to a recent accreditation report. The future-search conference helped to identify issues, capabilities, opportunities, and future directions. The competencies, skills, and intellectual capital developed as part of this search conference have had a significant impact on how the department is addressing its issues and challenges. Faculty and staff are more cognizant of how the decisions were made and what to expect in terms of actions and results. They also are more aware of the importance of developing requisite competencies at the organizational and individual levels, and of holding faculty and staff accountable for performance.

The outcomes of this future search have set the stage for closer integration between the academic department and the diagnostic laboratory in which clinical services are provided to clients. With the new strategic plan, both the department and the diagnostic laboratory have coordinated their efforts and are taking essential steps toward meeting the challenges facing the department.

Note

1. Future-search conferences were popularized by Marvin Weisbord in the mid-1980s, but they have a long history dating back to the action research process of Kurt Lewin and the open systems methods of Fred Emery and Eric Trist. For more information, see Weisbord, M., and others. *Discovering Common Ground: How Future Search Conferences Bring People Together to Achieve Breakthrough Innovation, Empowerment, Shared Vision and Collaborative Action.* San Francisco: Berrett-Koehler, 1993.

CHESTER C. WARZYNSKI is director of organizational development services and a lecturer in the Department of Human Resource Studies at Cornell University's School of Industrial and Labor Relations.

11

*Guided by clear planning principles, and under the
custodial care of a governance council, the model
strategic planning process at Carroll Community
College is evidence-driven, connected to budget
decisions, and continuously refreshed.*

Strategic Planning at Carroll Community College

Craig A. Clagett

Carroll Community College has developed a strategic planning process
designed to meet the needs of the college's various stakeholders, notably the
governing board, administrators, area and departmental planners, faculty,
and staff. Institutional research is a key contributor to this process. To mesh
with operational and budget planning cycles, strategic planning at Carroll
Community College employs a rolling two-year time frame. Although the
planning horizon and discussion context for given topics often extend further
than two years, the institution's strategic plan delineates, in each case,
specific tasks for completion within the subsequent two fiscal years.

At Carroll Community College, planning is:

- Guided by a set of planning standards
- Conducted by a collegewide Planning Advisory Council
- Facilitated by a continuously revised strategic plan
- Funded by the college budget
- Evaluated against a set of institutional effectiveness assessment measures

As a model for other institutions, I present a synopsis of these features.

Planning Standards

Planning at Carroll Community College adheres to seven standards:

1. Planning is guided by institutional vision.
2. Planning is informed by data.

3. All faculty and staff have the opportunity to participate in planning.
4. Budgeting reflects college priorities as identified in the strategic plan.
5. Area and office plans support the strategic plan.
6. Institutional effectiveness is assessed.
7. Assessment results are used for improvement.

At its final meeting of each academic year, the Planning Advisory Council evaluates the college's planning performance over the course of the year against these standards. All college personnel have the opportunity to conduct the same assessment as part of the college's biennial employee satisfaction survey. The institutional research office is responsible for processing both of these evaluations.

Planning Advisory Council

The Planning Advisory Council facilitates and guides planning at Carroll Community College. The council has twenty-seven members. Fifteen individuals are permanent members of the council by virtue of the positions they hold at the college and the nature of the administrative and planning responsibilities vested in these positions. The permanent members of the council are all four vice presidents, the associate vice president of student affairs, the executive assistant to the president, and the directors or executive directors of eight functional areas of the college. The administrative assistant to the vice president for planning, marketing, and assessment is a voting member of the council and serves as its secretary. Four of the college's six academic chairpersons serve on the council at a given time, on a rotating basis. Six members of the teaching faculty serve on the council, including the presidents of the academic council and the college senate. The final two voting members are a student appointed by the student government organization and a member of the college's board of trustees. The presence of a board member on the council helps ensure communication between the governing board and the chief planning body of the college.

Twenty-seven is a large membership compared to most committees at the college, and it exceeds the number usually recommended for effective group action, but the council's size has not precluded effective deliberation and decision making. Indeed, the Planning Advisory Council has grown to this size by the desire of members to be on the council, and the council's need to have certain functions regularly represented. The council meets in the college's board room, which accommodates the membership well. The college president is not a member of the Planning Advisory Council, since its role is to make recommendations to the president, but the president routinely attends council meetings and addresses the group.

The mission of the Planning Advisory Council encompasses several roles. Following the leadership of the president, the council promotes a vision for the future of the college and recommends strategic directions for realizing this vision. Both the vision and the strategic directions are rooted in the institution's mission and statement of purposes.

The Planning Advisory Council is the custodian of the college's strategic plan; it approves addition and deletion of task statements from the plan, monitors implementation of actions to fulfill the goals of the plan, and reports to the college community on the institution's progress in achieving its strategic initiatives.

The council established and maintains a system of institutional effectiveness assessment measures for monitoring college performance and reporting to stakeholders.

The council solicits, reviews, and disseminates analytical data describing the college and its environment, and it employs SWOT (strengths, weaknesses, opportunities, threats) analysis to identify the strategic assets and vulnerabilities of the college. The council annually endorses strategic initiatives for priority funding and serves as the college's budget committee. Requests for budget increases beyond inflation and volume increases must be justified in terms of the initiatives in the strategic plan or anticipated improvements in institutional effectiveness as measured by board-approved assessment measures.

The council evaluates institutional planning processes by reviewing area plans for congruence with the college's strategic priorities, approving institutionwide functional plans, and overseeing the activities of committees such as the Marketing Communications Advisory Group and the Technology Advisory Group.

Strategic Plan

The college uses its strategic plan to manage institutionwide planning. The strategic plan is not a glossy publication for external relations; instead, it is a working document that is altered numerous times each year. It contains ten or fewer strategic initiatives, plus supporting task statements to implement the strategic initiatives. The task statements include identification of the person(s) responsible for their completion and an expected completion date.

Strategic initiatives are added to the strategic plan by the president of the college in late June, following endorsement by the board of trustees. This annual announcement of the president's strategic initiatives may include revision to current initiatives in addition to new ones. Examples of presidential initiatives in recent years are "Incorporate diversity and global awareness into the curriculum and cocurricular activities" and "Institutionalize assessment into all areas of the college." The initiatives guide area annual planning for the coming year and budget development for the following year. For example, the initiatives announced in June 2003 will guide area, office, and employee goal setting for FY2004 and development of the FY2005 operating budget.

Following announcement of the president's strategic initiatives in June, area annual goal setting commences for the fiscal year beginning July 1. Each vice president is responsible for the planning processes in her or his area. Area goals in support of accomplishment of the president's strategic initiatives are furnished to the president by August 15 of each year. Area planning also includes process improvement, productivity enhancement, staff development, and other area mission-related goals not related directly to the president's initiatives. These are not included in the strategic plan but drive office and employee goal setting for the year. Area goals and task statements supportive of the president's strategic initiatives are shared by each vice president at the first meeting of the Planning Advisory Council in September. Once approved by the council, they become part of the institution's strategic plan.

The council appoints a strategic plan reporter for each strategic initiative at its first meeting in September. During September and October, the strategic plan reporter(s) for each strategic initiative review the task statements supporting their initiative to ensure that, collectively, the tasks effectively achieve the initiative. If the reporter feels additional tasks or coordination is necessary to accomplish the initiative, the reporter brings such recommendations to the Planning Advisory Council in November. The council may vote to add more task statements to the strategic plan throughout the year.

In the spring, the Planning Advisory Council oversees a mini-self-study process to assess the institution's progress on fulfilling the goals in the strategic plan.

By May 1, each vice president or designated reporter reviews the status of the task statements in her or his area and assigns to each of them one of these status descriptions:

- Retire—completed. The goal or action has been accomplished in full.
- Retire—assimilated. The goal or action has been incorporated into routine operations and funding.
- On schedule. Progress toward completing the goal or action is proceeding as planned.
- Behind schedule. Current progress toward completing the goal or action is less than planned.
- Delete—abandoned. The goal or action has been abandoned because of other priorities.
- Delete—subsumed. The goal or action has been subsumed into another task statement.

The status reports from each vice president or designated reporting person are compiled and shared with the Planning Advisory Council at its May meeting. The council votes to accept or reject proposed retirements and deletions from the strategic plan. Council-approved retirements and deletions are noted on the end-of-year version of the strategic plan, which is posted on the Carroll Community College intranet.

The reporters for each strategic initiative assess the level of achievement of their initiative during April and May of each year and present a status report to the Planning Advisory Council at the May meeting. These individual reports are compiled and included in the council's annual report. (This report also includes presentation of trend data for the institutional effectiveness assessment measures; this is discussed later.) Editing, formatting, and publication of the annual report are the responsibility of the planning, marketing, and assessment area. The council receives a draft of the report for review and officially adopts it at the last meeting of the year.

Strategic initiatives are retired from the strategic plan by the president, with the concurrence of the board of trustees. The date of retirement is noted on the end-of-year version of the strategic plan. Strategic initiatives from prior years may remain in the strategic plan if associated area goals and actions are still active.

Strategic Planning and the College Budget

Having area goals tied to strategic initiatives, which have been guided by institutional vision, approved by a governing board, and developed by consultation and consensus, is not enough. Resources must be allocated to adequately fund the tasks necessary to realize the goals of each initiative.

Carroll Community College has developed a process that ties its annual budget to the institution's strategic plan. The budget for the upcoming fiscal year (beginning July 1) is developed during the fall. After an initial presentation of budget assumptions and a review of the process at the Planning Advisory Council in September, campus departments and offices develop budget requests for the next fiscal year through their area planning processes. All requests for funds beyond inflation and volume increases to maintain current operations must be justified in terms of (1) the strategic initiatives in the current strategic plan or (2) their anticipated positive impact on one or more institutional effectiveness assessment measures. All requests for new monies are presented to the Planning Advisory Council in October, where vice presidents or their staff members make the case for each respective proposal.

Collectively, the area budget requests typically exceed available revenues for new initiatives. During October and November, the president's executive team and the Planning Advisory Council work through several versions of a balanced budget. In November, a proposed budget is presented to the college senate and the student government organization for comment, and then to the board of trustees along with supporting materials. The board acts on the budget in December, when, upon approval, it is submitted to the county government.

Institutional Effectiveness Assessment Measures

Carroll Community College is committed to ongoing assessment and evaluation of its programs and services, and to public documentation of institutional effectiveness to furnish accountability to its stakeholders.

College Statement of Purposes

Carroll Community College considers assessment an integral part of planning. At the strategic planning level, identifying measures of institutional effectiveness is deemed essential. Managers and stakeholders use these indicators to determine if the institution is successful in achieving its mission and moving itself forward. The indicators constitute a framework empowering unit-level planners to innovate by establishing stable expectations about what is really important. Likely improvement in specific indicators can be used to justify a request for new monies in the annual budget development process.

At the direction of the president, during spring 1999 the college's Planning Advisory Council developed a comprehensive program of institutional effectiveness assessment. This included a set of seventy-two institutional effectiveness assessment measures, forty-two of which were adopted by the board of trustees on June 21, 1999, as "core indicators" to promote public accountability by comparing results to purpose. These measures cover all areas of the institution's mission:

- Access and opportunity
- Student development and learning
- Baccalaureate preparation
- Workforce development
- The teaching and learning environment
- Community outreach and lifelong learning
- Resource development and use

The planning, marketing, and assessment area presents an annual institutional effectiveness report to the board at its annual retreat in January. The report is shared with the Planning Advisory Council in the spring, prior to consideration of strategic initiatives for the next two-year planning cycle.

Institutional research maintains the trend data for the institutional effectiveness assessment measures. The research office developed a crosswalk among these institutional effectiveness measures developed by the Planning Advisory Council and the performance accountability indicators mandated by the Maryland Higher Education Commission, the performance monitoring indicators supporting enrollment management, and the goals contained in the college's academic plan, student affairs plan, continuing education and training plan, marketing communications plan, and technology plan. As this suggests, Carroll Community College uses data to inform planning throughout the institution.

These institutional effectiveness measures are only one component of the college's comprehensive assessment and accountability program. Assessment of student learning outcomes and teaching effectiveness is the responsibility of the faculty and falls under the direction of the vice president of academic and student affairs. Other areas of the college also are engaged in program evaluation and additional assessment activities. The institutional research office supports all of these activities.

Conclusion

This chapter has presented the model strategic planning process used by Carroll Community College. Guided by clear planning principles, and under the custodial care of a governance council, the process at this institution is evidence-driven, connected to budget decisions, and continuously refreshed. At many community colleges, institutional research and planning are combined in one unit (sometimes one person). This facilitates use of data and research findings to guide and assess campus planning activities. At Carroll, the institutional research office reports to the vice president in charge of strategic planning. At other institutions, the institutional research officer may be the chief planning officer. Planning and institutional research are so intertwined at most community colleges that the American Association of Community Colleges has one council for both functions, the National Council for Research and Planning.

Use of institutional effectiveness assessment measures or key performance indicators raises the importance of the office of institutional research in strategic planning. As planning and budgeting become more reliant on performance indicators—a relationship increasingly expected by accreditation commissions—the role of institutional research becomes increasingly critical.

CRAIG A. CLAGETT *has been vice president for planning, marketing, and assessment at Carroll Community College since 1998.*

*The author describes practical steps for infusing the
strategic plan throughout the organization. These steps
have carried the University of Wisconsin–Madison
effectively through two cycles of reaccreditation and
planning.*

Moving the Strategic Plan off the Shelf and into Action at the University of Wisconsin–Madison

Kathleen A. Paris

"The most radical thing I did was to take a plan off the shelf and implement
it." So David Ward, now president of the American Council on Education,
described how he began cultivating strategic planning at the University of
Wisconsin–Madison in 1991 during his tenure as provost. The plan, *Future
Directions,* indicated that undergraduate education was in need of attention.
For the next three years, Ward focused resources on improving the undergraduate experience, along with five other priorities. The strategic plan in
action yielded a number of innovations, notably cross-college academic
advising for students who had not yet selected majors, transformation of
residence halls into learning communities with close ties to faculty, and
both classroom and community learning opportunities.

Upon becoming chancellor in 1993, Ward made *Future Directions* the
foundation of his agenda. Significantly, the publication was the product of
the North Central Association (NCA) reaccreditation process. It was written by members of the faculty and administration and distilled the themes
of the reaccreditation report and implications for the future of UW-
Madison. So successful was the experience of using the reaccreditation
study results as the framework of the campus plan that the pattern was
repeated for the 1999 NCA reaccreditation process. Figure 12.1 shows that
UW-Madison has completed the second iteration of the process that builds
the campus plan on the reaccreditation outcomes.

The accreditation-to-plan model is effective on several levels. First, the
accreditation self-study is a massive process that involves input and feedback

Figure 12.1. Two Cycles of Reaccreditation and Strategic Planning at UW–Madison

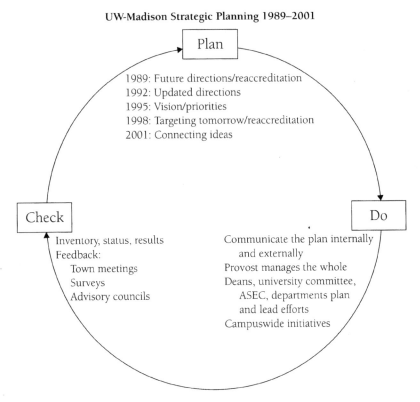

UW-Madison Strategic Planning 1989–2001

Plan

1989: Future directions/reaccreditation
1992: Updated directions
1995: Vision/priorities
1998: Targeting tomorrow/reaccreditation
2001: Connecting ideas

Check

Inventory, status, results
Feedback:
   Town meetings
   Surveys
   Advisory councils

Do

Communicate the plan internally
   and externally
Provost manages the whole
Deans, university committee,
   ASEC, departments plan
   and lead efforts
Campuswide initiatives

from all levels of the campus and from internal and external constituencies. Why not immediately use the data on strengths, limitations, opportunities, threats, and trends to craft a dynamic and meaningful plan? The alternative is to use similar organizational resources to duplicate a comparable process of campus involvement, or involve far fewer internal and external stakeholders in creating a strategic plan at another time.

Second, the process by which the campus strategic plan is developed strongly influences how fully it is implemented. Using the information and recommendations emerging from reaccreditation helps ensure that the faculty and staff who ultimately implement the plan understand the problems and aims that undergird it. In UW-Madison's 1999 reaccreditation process, almost three hundred faculty, staff, and students served on committees or focus groups to create the self-study. This meant that a substantial group of opinion leaders who had demonstrated their commitment to the institution through participation in reaccreditation were already familiar with many of the issues and goals contained in the plan.

Pull Versus Push

Readers are keenly aware of the aspects of higher education that mitigate against implementing an organizationwide plan: decentralized structures, specialization, the independent and entrepreneurial culture of the academic department, a tradition of discrete silos, and abhorrence of private sector business jargon. Given these realities, the University of Wisconsin–Madison has approached planning and implementation as a "pull" rather than a "push." Maury Cotter, who directs the Office of Quality Improvement and serves on both the chancellor's and provost's staff, says, "The strategic plan serves as a magnet, drawing people toward a desirable future. Those who are compelled to help create that future participate voluntarily, bringing their own creative ideas and commitment."

Communication

Communication about the plan and what it means for the organization is necessary, although not sufficient alone. The core of UW-Madison's strategic plan is the mission, vision (ultimate objective for the future), and priorities shown in Figure 12.2. The priorities are explained in detail with examples in the form of "tree diagrams" on the chancellor's Web site (Wiley, 2004)).

Figure 12.2. UW–Madison Mission, Vision, and Priorities, 2003

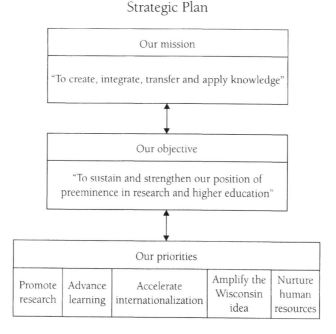

For example, the tree for "improve learning—graduate and professional education" includes the goal "Assure that graduates have the set of skills appropriate for the challenges and evolving needs of their early careers." The "branches" include examples such as establishing an office for graduate student professional development and promoting campuswide opportunities for developing graduate student teaching skills (such as the university's Center for the Integration of Research, Teaching, and Learning, and an NSF-funded K–12 development project).

When campus officials speak at any venue, the campus plan is always close at hand.

In addition to the planning documents on the Web and in hard copy, one-page versions of the mission, vision, and priorities were produced and are made available to a variety of internal and external audiences at learning events, advisory board meetings, development events, visits by accrediting bodies, and the like. A pocket-sized version of the plan has been well received. Every year, a progress update on the plan is produced and disseminated online and in hard copy to all faculty, staff, and external constituents. The regular updates illustrate the institution's commitment to using the plan to guide action and resource allocation.

Infusion Strategies

For the plan to be taken seriously, faculty, staff, and students must see it infused throughout the organization. It must be part of routine academic life. Here are specific infusion strategies taken at UW-Madison.

Identify Point People to Champion the Priorities. Official "point people" are assigned for each of the plan priorities. Point people are those whose positions are most associated with the priorities. For example, the point for research is the vice-chancellor for research and dean of the graduate school. The point for "accelerating internationalization" is the dean for international studies. Point person responsibilities include developing the overall strategy, coordinating the whole, clarifying roles and responsibilities, creating linkages, and monitoring and reporting on progress. Given the cross-functional nature of most of the priorities, point people are not likely to have functional authority over all of the players whose efforts they seek to coordinate. Essential skills of a point person are the ability to communicate across the silos and to focus people toward a common goal.

Create Key Positions Around Some of the Priorities. In some cases, associate vice-chancellor positions have been created and defined according to the campus plan priorities. (Associate vice-chancellors are respected faculty members who serve for approximately three to five years while continuing their faculty duties part-time.) Currently, associate vice-chancellors have responsibility for the plan priorities to advance learning and nurture human resources that encompass diversity.

Report According to the Plan. Deans and administrative division heads (student affairs, administration, and so forth) are asked to give the provost an annual reporting of activities organized according to the campus priorities. These reports provide much of the data for the annual institutionwide progress reports. As of fall 2003, examples were being extracted from these reports and expanded for feature in a regular column in the campus publication, *Wisconsin Week*.

The deans' council meeting agendas are designed to advance the campus priorities, including a comprehensive overview at their annual retreat. At their biweekly meetings, deans share effective practices and identify high-leverage opportunities for advancing the priorities.

The model used by the Office of Quality Improvement to facilitate strategic planning in academic departments and administrative offices as well as schools and colleges includes the question, "How do our activities support the priorities in the campus strategic plan?" This exercise helps participants recognize existing alignment with the plan as well as opportunities to align activities more closely with the overall plan. (For more information on this model, see Paris, 2002).

Allocate Discretionary Funds in Line with the Plan. Discretionary monies from the chancellor, provost, and deans are allocated almost exclusively to efforts capable of showing that their successful accomplishment will directly advance the campus plan and priorities.

Consider Plan Priorities When Facing Budget Reductions. The fiscal situation in the state of Wisconsin became particularly difficult beginning in the fall of 2002; the university was affected significantly by budget cuts intended to address the state's budget deficit. Deans and directors were given suggested guidelines for making budget decisions and were encouraged by the chancellor and provost to consider the plan priorities in deciding what to protect and what to cut. They were encouraged to ask, "To what extent is the function, program, service, or unit a priority in the campus strategic plan?" Centrality to the plan was a key criterion for budget decision making ("Strategies for Discussing Budget Priorities," 2003).

Spotlight Plan at High-Visibility Campus Events. When UW-Madison celebrated its 150th birthday in 1999, the plan priorities were the major themes of the event and accomplishments were highlighted in a campus showcase of accomplishments. A progress report on the campus plan was released as part of the sesquicentennial activity.

Provide Academic Leadership Training and Development to Support Plan. The campus plan and priorities customarily figure prominently in learning events offered to department chairs, managers, supervisors, and other academic leaders. Significantly, the campus leaders who take part in these learning events are not only acquainted (or reacquainted) with the priorities; they are given tools, techniques, and opportunities to develop their skills in advancing those priorities.

A new online system that automatically notifies faculty and staff of professional development activities of interest to them (on the basis of their preferences) enables faculty and staff to search for learning events according to the campus priority. Point people can monitor which learning opportunities are available for campus priorities and where gaps may exist. This online resource is itself a direct outcome of the campus priority to "nurture human resources" ("My Professional Development," 2003).

Tie Academic Program Reviews to Plan. Letters and Science, the largest college on the UW-Madison campus, requires academic programs preparing for program review to describe activities according to the campus plan priorities: "The process of program review provides departments with an opportunity to engage in meaningful planning as well as to align the many ways in which their work serves the broader goals of the College and University. To facilitate that understanding, the questions. . . . are arranged in concert with the five goals described in 'Connecting Ideas,' UW-Madison's strategic plan" ("Academic Program Review," 2003).

Summary

The examples described here suggest that the campus strategic plan and priorities are infused, at many points, into the life of the campus. Commenting on the challenges of the future and the capacity of UW-Madison to maintain its leading edge in creating and disseminating new knowledge, Chancellor John Wiley has said: "The answer, I believe, lies within our strategic planning process, which for the past decade has been a key component of the University's progress. Strategic planning is an invaluable process for identifying strengths and weaknesses, pointing out critical needs, and helping determine how best to meet those needs. In the past, solid planning has helped us overcome many obstacles and has given us the tools to protect and enhance the valuable resources of the university. Now, as we face new opportunities for growth, it remains crucial to our future success" (Wiley, 2001, n.p.)

References

"Academic Program Review." University of Wisconsin–Madison, College of Letters and Science, Sep. 2003. http://www.ls.wisc.edu/handbook/ChapterFive/chV-4.htm, retrieved Sep. 21, 2004.

"My Professional Development." University of Wisconsin–Madison, 2003. http://www.myprofdev.wisc.edu, retrieved Sep. 21, 2004.

Paris, K. A. "Strategic Planning in the University." Office of Quality Improvement, University of Wisconsin–Madison, 2002.

http://www.wisc.edu/improve/strplan/collection.pdf, retrieved Sep. 18, 2004.

"Strategies for Discussing Budget Priorities and Reductions." University of Wisconsin–Madison, Mar. 14, 2003. http://www.provost.wisc.edu/docs/strat.pdf, retrieved Sep. 21, 2004.

Wiley, J. D. "A One-Year Progress Report on the Strategic Plan." University of Wisconsin–Madison, 2001. http://www.chancellor.wisc.edu/strategicplan/progress.html, retrieved Sep. 18, 2004.

Wiley, J. D. "Connecting Ideas and Strategies for the University of Wisconsin–Madison." University of Wisconsin–Madison, Sep. 2004. http://www.chancellor.wisc.edu/strategicplan/, retrieved Sep. 21, 2004.

KATHLEEN A. PARIS, *now a consultant, is a distinguished emeritus member of the Office of Quality Improvement, University of Wisconsin–Madison.*

This chapter summarizes several strategic planning models, identifies the top ten planning tools, and presents an annotated "pick six" of key strategic planning references.

Models and Tools for Strategic Planning

James F. Trainer

Each of the preceding chapters and case studies contributes in its own way to the fourfold objectives for this volume. The first objective seeks to introduce strategic planning in higher education. Although many planning and institutional research staff are well versed in statistics and social science research methodologies—skills that are useful in support of planning—surprisingly few have formal training in strategic planning itself. As a second objective, the editors and authors have demonstrated the use of a variety of strategic planning models and methodologies, which institutional researchers may elect to employ in support of planning efforts on their campuses. Third, we focus on plan implementation rather than simply on planning, as an activity in and of itself. Critics believe that planning has focused too heavily on the process of developing a plan rather than on implementation or outcome of the plan. The final objective has been to encourage planning and institutional research staff to identify and seek out opportunities to engage in and support the planning processes.

In meeting the objectives of this volume, the first chapter creates a foundation for strategic planning, particularly in higher education. By developing the historical chronology of strategic planning and defining its terms and concepts, the chapter dispels the mystique of planning and opens the way for digesting the rest of the volume.

Chapter Two is the first of several in this volume that link strategic planning with accreditation. Accreditation bodies increasingly force institutions to merge their accountability reporting, institutional research, outcomes assessment, and decision-making activities; several of the case study institutions began their planning efforts only after a negative accreditation review. We also learn in Chapter Two that the Malcolm Baldrige continuous improvement framework supports a systems perspective and a focus on results.

Chapter Three extends this discussion and identifies eleven lessons learned from Baldrige-recognized best-practice organizations.

Chapter Four presents three case examples of how ad hoc requests for seemingly routine institutional research information can be converted into an opportunity that informs longer-term planning.

Chapter Five describes the external and internal forces that are stimulating institutions to create and link offices and positions that specialize in planning, quality improvement, and institutional research.

Chapter Six further illuminates the links among planning, quality assurance, and institutional research at the new Ellis Island, Los Angeles City College, where a negative accreditation review provoked establishment of a planning process that is successfully creating a culture of continuous improvement.

Chapter Seven depicts an institution where a financial model is the centerpiece of strategic planning.

Chapter Eight reinforces integration of planning across several areas of the university, among them enrollment, budgeting, physical plant, and staffing.

Chapter Nine explores and defends the use of teams in plan implementation and goal attainment, thus moving the institution from planning to action.

Chapter Ten introduces a specific participatory planning technique, future-search conferencing, which creates greater understanding, coordination, and commitment.

Chapter Eleven presents a model strategic planning process that is evidence-driven, connected to budget decisions, and continuously refreshed.

Chapter Twelve pays specific attention to plan implementation, monitoring, and integration with institutional reaccreditation, thus infusing the strategic plan throughout the organization.

This final chapter helps planners and institutional researchers identify opportunities to participate in strategic planning by examining several strategic planning models, as well as the natural intersections of various institutional research and planning activities. The chapter also features an annotated list of top-ten planning tools. Finally, the chapter closes with a "pick six" list of references on strategic planning, which institutional researchers may want to consult as they venture into the planning arena.

Strategic Planning Models

This volume contains a number of helpful strategic planning models. The value of a model is that it serves as a logic chart to guide the process. A model not only permits organizational clarity but also conserves

Figure 13.1. Basic Elements of the Strategic Management Process

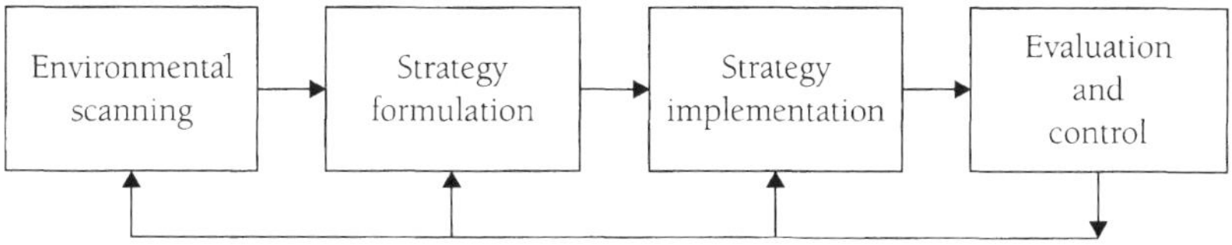

workload by focusing attention on the most important planning activities and processes.

In Chapter Two, Ann Dodd integrates accreditation, planning, assessment, and improvement initiatives by placing them within a simple input-process-output (IPO) model. Institutional effectiveness and accountability are viewed as outcomes of the IPO model, and a feedback loop affords continuous improvement. She also displays a model showing the continuous cycle of planning, assessment, and improvement at Penn State University. This model grew out of a TQM initiative and is a forerunner of the Baldrige model that is also examined in her chapter. In Chapter Three, Jasinski further discusses the organizational systems model that guides the Baldrige performance program.

In Chapter Six, Seymour describes the effective master planning model at Los Angeles City College. This elaborate model features plan-act-check components for both strategic (long-term) and operational (short-term) levels. Chapter Twelve contains a similar plan-do-check model that organizes the practical implementation of the University of Wisconsin's mission, objectives, and priorities. The models in these chapters lay out planning roadmaps for readers of this volume.

Hunger and Wheelen (2003) suggest that all strategic planning (now quite often referred to, as it is by these authors, as strategic management) involves at least four distinct steps: environmental scanning, strategy formulation, strategy implementation, and evaluation and control. These steps are portrayed in the model presented in Figure 13.1 (Hunger and Wheelen, 2003).

More recently, Michael Dooris and his colleagues at Penn State University present two additional ways to view strategic planning and the role of institutional research within it. The first, as demonstrated in Figure 13.2, examines the relationship between measurement (a concept familiar to all institutional researchers) and the various steps of the strategic planning, implementation, and evaluation process.

The second model emanating from Penn State proposes that institutional researchers think about the intersection of planning and assessment and institutional improvement activities. This model is highlighted in the concentric circles of a Venn diagram, in Figure 13.3. Mission, vision, values, and goals of the unit or organization lie at the intersection of these

Figure 13.2. Linking the Measurement System

Performance

Mission, vision, values

Goals

Strategic performance indicators (key strategies)

Measures of performance

Targets

Processes   Actions

Data and improvement

Source: Penn State University, Office of Planning and Institutional Assessment.

Figure 13.3. Integrating Planning, Assessment, and Improvement Within Units

Planning

Mission, vision, values, goals

Improvement   Assessment

Source: Penn State University, Office of Planning and Institutional Assessment.

activities and ought to drive all that we do to support these efforts from an institutional research perspective. However, when Penn State's IR and planning staff members work with units, they often discourage departments from beginning with a visioning exercise, or with a group attempt to craft and edit a mission statement. This is an important practical point. In Penn State's experience, there is a huge distinction between placing mission and vision at the center of planning, assessment, and improvement—an idea that makes sense to administrators, faculty, and staff—and attempting to start a planning process by writing a perfect mission statement as a group. Such an effort can be a frustrating and time-consuming energy drain.

So, given these models, where might the institutional researcher begin to engage the strategic planning process? Clearly, there is a role within strategic planning for the institutional researcher, as shown in the models by Dodd, Baldrige, Dooris, Hunger and Wheelen, Jasinski, Paris, and Seymour. Whether one sees strategic planning as a four- or six-step progression, or as an ongoing cyclical process that periodically scans the external environment and matches it against internal reality, it is clear that there are many opportunities for institutional researchers to connect to, engage in, and facilitate the process. Environmental scanning is crucial at the beginning of any planning process, and feedback at the end is clearly an important aspect of every planning model. Both give institutional research a prominent role in the strategic planning process. Good institutional research is also needed for benchmarking against peer competitors, analyzing the student admissions pool, projecting enrollments and revenues, studying salaries and turnover, assessing student and alumni outcomes, gathering demographic and economic forecasts, monitoring the use of space and facilities, and evaluating the impact of programs and policies. These are all directly related to effective strategic planning and constitute a challenging agenda for institutional researchers. In addition, several of these models foster the opportunity for institutional researchers to develop and track key performance indicators and targets, something that institutional researchers are well prepared to do. We suggest that there may also be a role for institutional researchers in facilitating that part of the process where goals, strategies, and plans are formulated. It is with these opportunities in mind that we turn our attention to our top ten strategic planning tools.

Top Ten Planning Tools

Our top ten may prove useful to institutional researchers as they participate in or facilitate the strategic planning processes at their institution. By no means is the list comprehensive and exhaustive, and these are not meant to provide step-by-step procedures for employing any one of these tools. Rather, the list introduces readers to important resources they may wish to explore in detail with information from elsewhere. The section on resources for strategic planning, which follows the list, has a number of suggestions of texts that the institutional researcher interested in building her or his planning repertoire may want to pursue in depth. Of course, others may develop quite a different list of both planning tools and resources from those suggested here. However, on the basis of the collective experience of the editors of this volume, we believe these are among the best available. Obviously, each of the tools and references suggested here has its own strengths and weaknesses.

1. *SWOT analysis.* The SWOT analysis (strengths, weaknesses, opportunities, and threats) lies at the heart of strategic planning. One of the most

familiar of all strategic planning tools, SWOT analysis assesses campus competitiveness by revealing the alignment between the institution's resources and programs versus its external environment. The "strategic" part of strategic planning involves capturing and maintaining a market niche in the competition for resources, faculty, and students, and SWOT analysis makes this possible. SWOT analysis is designed to facilitate the environmental scanning component of strategic planning by asking those participating in developing the plan to think about the context in which a given organization functions and to assess the competition. Strengths and weaknesses are internal or inherent to the organization, whereas opportunities and threats are external. Any of a number of techniques (for example, brainstorming, nominal group, multiple voting, various types of data collection and analysis) can be employed in conducting a SWOT analysis, but it is all about understanding the competitive environment in which an organization exists, and it has internal and external faces.

2. *TOWS analysis.* A TOWS analysis, or matrix, can be thought of as the corollary or reciprocal of the SWOT analysis. TOWS stands for "Turning Opportunities and Weaknesses into Strengths." When employing a TOWS analysis, one creates a classic two-by-two table with four cells. Data, or lists, generated in a SWOT analysis are then viewed through the lens of the TOWS matrix. The four cells that are formed allow planners to think about strategies, as Hunger and Wheelen (2003) point out, that take strengths and turn them into opportunities (*so*), that employ strengths to avoid or avert threats (*st*), that attempt to take advantage of opportunities by overcoming weaknesses (*wo*), and that act to minimize weaknesses and avoid threats (*wt*).

3. *Nominal group technique.* The nominal group technique is a brainstorming technique whereby a group is a group, at least initially, in name only. All participants are asked to work alone, in silence, in generating their individual brainstorming list in response to the initial prompt (question or instruction leading to development of a list of responses, e.g., "Develop a list of what you think are the most pressing issues facing our organization today"). Once everyone has had sufficient time to develop an individual list, participants are asked, again working alone, to attempt to rank-order or prioritize the items on their list and to select some portion of them (top half, top quarter, and so on). After everyone has had the opportunity to prioritize his or her own list, a round-robin technique is employed whereby the facilitator goes around the room and asks each participant to identify the top item, placing them on a common list. If, when a participant is reached, the person's top item is already on the list, the participant can then offer the next item on the list. This procedure continues until the participants and facilitator agree that all of the pertinent items have been placed on the common list. Subsequent to development of the common list, any of a number of techniques, such as multiple voting, can be used to cull and prioritize the common list.

4. *Affinity diagrams.* An affinity diagram is like the nominal group technique in that participants begin the process by working on their own. In the case of the affinity diagram, they silently write ideas related to the topic at hand on Post-It notes (only one per note) and then place the notes on the wall or some other flat surface. Once all the ideas are on the wall, the participants, still working in silence, begin to move the notes around to group similar ideas together. After the notes have been arranged into categories, the group as a whole discusses the themes that have emerged.

5. *SMART language.* SMART is an acronym for *specific, measurable, achievable or attainable, results-oriented,* and *time-bound.* SMART language should be employed when writing strategic goals, especially at the unit level. Using SMART language should help avoid developing goals that are too general, vague, and platitudinous.

6. *Responsibility matrix.* A responsibility matrix is simply a tool to help keep track of who is taking responsibility for certain actions and steps in the implementation of a plan. In a sense, it is means of maintaining accountability and tracking process. The matrix lists in the rows specific tasks, while the columns include information on the person, party, or office responsible for taking the action as well as possible substeps in the process and target dates for having completed the task. Chapters Seven, Eight, and Nine in this volume contain examples of a responsibility matrix of sorts.

7. *Flowcharting.* Flowcharts portray how the steps of a process or plan fit together and relate to one another. Agreed-on shapes (ovals, rectangles, diamonds, and so on) are employed to depict the various step types involved in the process or plan. Lines and arrows indicate the direction and order of the steps. Usually, ovals note the start and finishing points of the process, rectangles depict specific steps, and diamonds indicate a point at which a decision must be made or an option executed. Most flowcharts also indicate the existence of feedback loops. Flowcharts are particularly helpful when plans have to be followed sequentially; when there are decision points along the way that, once executed, lead to other potential outcomes; and when it is necessary to identify and remedy potential problems in plan implementation.

8. *Cause-and-effect diagrams.* Cause-and-effect diagrams are also known as fishbone diagrams (thanks to their appearance; when complete, they look like the skeleton of a fish) or Ishikawa diagrams (named after the gentleman who first created them). They are a graphical representation of the various factors influencing a particular outcome, be it a problem or a desired result. They are particularly useful in identifying and organizing the potential causes of a given effect, in isolating potential causes of variation in a process or outcome, in ascertaining the actions needed to produce a desired effect, and in determining the potential consequences of implementing a selected course of action. You create the diagram by first identifying the potential outcome and placing it in a rectangle on the right-hand side of a sheet of paper arranged horizontally. You then draw a horizon line,

connecting to the effect box, off to the left of the box; this line becomes the "backbone" of the "fish." Diagonal lines or "ribs" drawn off the spine link to other rectangles, which are used to identify the major categories of cause of the effect. Lines coming off the ribs indicate possible items and specifics related to the root causes of an effect. The diagram is fleshed out by continuously asking why a certain item affects the outcome in a particular way.

9. *Presentation of quantitative data.* It behooves any researcher responsible for gathering and presenting quantitative data as part of, in support of, or in monitoring implementation of a strategic planning initiative to be skilled in presenting quantitative findings. The value of even the best research design, administration, collection, and analysis can be diminished if the results of a study are incomprehensible to the audience for whom they are being produced. In addition to being a skilled researcher and writer, individuals called on to support the planning process with quantitative data will want to produce first-rate tables, charts, and graphs. Readers are encouraged to consult the work of Edward Tufte on presentation of quantitative data, as well as the publication *Effective Reporting* by Trudy Bers and Jeffery Seybert (published by AIR, 2001).

10. *Goal attainment teams.* Developing, implementing, and monitoring strategic plans are all wonderful opportunities to engage the members and stakeholders of an organization in shaping and realizing the vision and goals of their shared enterprise. Indeed, a number of the planning tools described here and throughout this volume suggest the involvement of a variety of individuals in the planning process. As noted in Chapter Nine, Villanova University has been particularly successful in engaging teams in developing and monitoring key performance indicators related to strategic goals. Hallmarks of the team approach include engaging members of the organization in the planning process; identifying and using expertise from across the enterprise in the planning, plan implementation, and plan monitoring processes; and developing a sense of ownership of and commitment to the plan and its implementation.

A "Pick Six" of Planning Resources and References

The references listed here are a good starting point for the institutional researcher wishing to gain a better understanding of the strategic planning process and the context in which it occurs, as well as the resources available to support planning efforts.

Academic Strategy: The Management Revolution in American Higher Education, by George Keller (Johns Hopkins Press, 1983).
　　Although more than twenty years old, Keller's text remains a seminal work on strategy formulation in higher education. It is a nice introduction to the notion and evolution of planning within the context of the academy. The text is mainly conceptual, rather than pragmatic in nature.

A Guide for New Planners, by Donald M. Norris and Nick L. Poulton (Society for College and University Planning, 1991).

Published by the preeminent organization of college and university planners, this guide presents a number of conceptual frameworks, analytical tools, and worksheets that should prove useful to the college planner. It also features a roadmap to the planning literature as it stood in 1991.

Strategic Planning for Public and Nonprofit Organizations: A Guide to Strengthening and Sustaining Organizational Achievement (rev. ed.), by John M. Bryson (Jossey-Bass, 1995).

A classic comprehensive guide to planning in the nonprofit sector, this book introduces the strategic change cycle and focuses on identifying strategic issues and developing strategies and plans to address them. The book also discusses the important role of leadership in the planning and implementation processes. A significant portion of the text is dedicated to describing resources that can be employed in the planning process.

Strategic Planning in Higher Education: Theory and Practice, by Robert A. Sevier (Council for the Advancement and Support of Education, 2000).

Following an introduction to the changing environment of higher education, the need for planning, the impact of organizational culture on planning, and the role of leadership in facilitating planning, this volume sets out a clear, step-by-step approach to the planning process. The appendices include sample documents, a list of terms and definitions, a directory of resources, and a case study.

Essentials of Strategic Management (3rd ed.), by J. David Hunger and Thomas L. Wheelen (Prentice Hall, 2003).

This volume offers a concise, pragmatic, yet detailed introduction to the concept and steps involved in strategic management. Though geared more toward corporations and for-profit enterprises, it nonetheless supplies a wealth of information and ideas that should prove helpful to the planner in higher education.

Field Guide to Nonprofit Strategic Planning and Facilitation, by Carter McNamara (Authenticity Consulting, 2003).

This is a practical how-to guide to strategic planning in nonprofit and charitable organizations. It is not specific to higher education, but it is particularly strong in identifying, following, and detailing the steps of the planning process. It begins with a section on planning to plan and includes a wealth of planning resources and worksheets. It has as a particular focus (and dedicates a major portion of the volume to) the role of the facilitator in the planning process. It is a useful guide to anyone who may be called on to facilitate the planning process in any nonprofit entity.

Conclusion

For the reader, this volume of *New Directions for Institutional Research* presents recurring themes: organizational alignment with strategic priorities, collaborative participatory processes, integrated systems thinking, evidence-based decisions, continuous improvement, and connectedness to accreditation and accountability. Our authors develop these themes across a rich array of public and private research universities, four-year campuses, and two-year colleges. We have displayed a collection of strategic planning models and identified a list of readings and resources. Thus armed, we trust that planners and researchers will use the contents of this volume to enhance the effectiveness of their institution.

JAMES F. TRAINER *is director of planning and assessment at Villanova University.*

INDEX

Back Issue/Subscription Order Form

Copy or detach and send to:

Jossey-Bass, A Wiley Imprint, 989 Market Street, San Francisco CA 94103-1741

Call or fax toll-free: Phone 888-378-2537 6:30AM – 3PM PST; Fax 888-481-2665

Back Issues: Please send me the following issues at $29 each
(Important: please include ISBN number with your order.)

_____

_____

_____

$ _____ Total for single issues

$ _____ SHIPPING CHARGES: SURFACE Domestic Canadian
First Item $5.00 $6.00
Each Add'l Item $3.00 $1.50
For next-day and second-day delivery rates, call the number listed above.

Subscriptions Please __ start __ renew my subscription to *New Directions for Institutional Research* for the year 2_____ at the following rate:

U.S.	__ Individual $80	__ Institutional $160
Canada	__ Individual $80	__ Institutional $200
All Others	__ Individual $104	__ Institutional $234
Online Subscription		__ Institutional $160

**For more information about online subscriptions visit
www.wileyinterscience.com**

$ _____ Total single issues and subscriptions (Add appropriate sales tax for your state for single issue orders. No sales tax for U.S. subscriptions. Canadian residents, add GST for subscriptions and single issues.)

__Payment enclosed (U.S. check or money order only)
__VISA __ MC __ AmEx # _____ Exp. Date _____

Signature _____ Day Phone _____
__ Bill Me (U.S. institutional orders only. Purchase order required.)

Purchase order # _____
Federal Tax ID13559302   **GST 89102 8052**

Name _____

Address _____

_____

Phone _____ E-mail _____

For more information about Jossey-Bass, visit our Web site at www.josseybass.com

OTHER TITLES AVAILABLE IN THE
NEW DIRECTIONS FOR INSTITUTIONAL RESEARCH SERIES
J. Fredericks Volkwein, Editor-in-Chief

IR122 **Assessing Character Outcomes in College**
Jon C. Dalton, Terrence R. Russell, Sally Kline
Examines several perspectives on the role of higher education in developing
students' character, and illustrates approaches to defining and assessing
character outcomes. Moral, civic, ethical, and spiritual development are key
aspects of students' growth and experience in college, so how can educators
encourage good values and assess their impact?
ISBN: 0-7879-7791-8

IR121 **Overcoming Survey Research Problems**
Stephen R. Porter
As demand for survey research has increased, survey response rates have
decreased. This volume examines an array of survey research problems and
best practices, from both the literature and field practitioners, to provide
solutions to increase response rates while controlling costs. Discusses
administering longitudinal studies, doing surveys on sensitive topics such as
student drug and alcohol use, and using new technologies for survey
administration.
ISBN: 0-7879-7477-3

IR120 **Using Geographic Information Systems in Institutional Research**
Daniel Teodorescu
Exploring the potential of geographic information systems (GIS) applications in
higher education administration, this issue introduces IR professionals and
campus administrators to a powerful presentation and analysis tool. Chapters
explore the benefits of working with the spatial component of data in
recruitment, admissions, facilities, alumni development, and other areas, with
examples of actual GIS applications from several higher education institutions.
ISBN: 0-7879-7281-9

IR119 **Maximizing Revenue in Higher Education**
F. King Alexander, Ronald G. Ehrenberg
This volume presents edited versions of some of the best articles from a forum
on institutional revenue generation sponsored by the Cornell Higher Education
Research Institute. The chapters provide different perspectives on revenue
generation and how institutions are struggling to find an appropriate balance
between meeting public expectations and maximizing private market forces.
The insights provided about options and alternatives will enable campus
leaders, institutional researchers, and policymakers to better understand
evolving patterns in public and private revenue reliance.
ISBN: 0-7879-7221-5

IR118 **Studying Diverse Institutions: Contexts, Challenges, and Considerations**
M. Christopher Brown II, Jason E. Lane
This volume examines the contextual and methodological issues pertaining to
studying diverse institutions (including women's colleges, tribal colleges, and
military academies), and provides effective and useful approaches for higher
education administrators, institutional researchers and planners, policymakers,
and faculty seeking to better understand students in postsecondary education.
It also offers guidelines to asking the right research questions, employing the
appropriate research design and methods, and analyzing the data with respect
to the unique institutional contexts.
ISBN: 0-7879-6990-7

Get Online Access to
New Directions for Institutional Research

New Directions for Institutional Research is available through Wiley InterScience, the dynamic online content service from John Wiley & Sons. Visit our Web site and enjoy a range of extremely useful features:

WILEY INTERSCIENCE ALERTS
   Content Alerts: Receive tables of contents alerts via e-mail as soon as a new issue is online.
   Profiled Alerts: Set up your own e-mail alerts based on personal queries, keywords, and other parameters.

WILEY
InterScience®
www.interscience.wiley.com
Discover something great

QUICK AND POWERFUL SEARCHING
   Browse and Search functions are designed to lead you to the information you need quickly and easily. Whether searching by title, keyword, or author, your results will point directly to the journal article, book chapter, encyclopedia entry or database you seek.

PERSONAL HOME PAGE
   Store and manage Wiley InterScience Alerts, searches, and links to key journals and articles.

MOBILEEDITION™
   Download table of contents and abstracts to your PDA every time you synchronize.

CROSSREF®
   Move seamlessly from a reference in a journal article to the cited journal articles, which may be located on a different server and published by a different publisher.

LINKS
   Navigate to and from indexing and abstracting services.

For more information about online access, please contact us at: North,Central, and South America: 1-800-511-3989, uscs-wis@wiley.com
All other regions: (+44) (0) 1243-843-345, cs-wis@wiley.co.uk

www.interscience.wiley.com

United States Postal Service

Statement of Ownership, Management, and Circulation

1. Publication Title	2. Publication Number	3. Filing Date
New Directions For Institutional Research	0 2 7 1 – 0 5 7 9	10/1/04

4. Issue Frequency	5. Number of Issues Published Annually	6. Annual Subscription Price
Quarterly	4	$160.00

7. Complete Mailing Address of Known Office of Publication (Not printer) (Street, city, county, state, and ZIP+4)

Wiley Subscription Services, Inc. at Jossey-Bass, 989 Market Street, San Francisco, CA 94103

Contact Person
Joe Schuman
Telephone
(415) 782-3232

8. Complete Mailing Address of Headquarters or General Business Office of Publisher (Not printer)

Wiley Subscription Services, Inc. 111 River Street, Hoboken, NJ 07030

9. Full Names and Complete Mailing Addresses of Publisher, Editor, and Managing Editor (Do not leave blank)

Publisher (Name and complete mailing address)

Wiley, San Francisco, 989 Market Street, San Francisco, CA 94103-1741

Editor (Name and complete mailing address)

J. Fredericks Volkwein, Penn State Univ./Center For Study of Higher Educ., 400 Rackley Bldg., University Park, PA 16801

Managing Editor (Name and complete mailing address)

None

10. Owner (Do not leave blank. If the publication is owned by a corporation, give the name and address of the corporation immediately followed by the names and addresses of all stockholders owning or holding 1 percent or more of the total amount of stock. If not owned by a corporation, give the names and addresses of the individual owners. If owned by a partnership or other unincorporated firm, give its name and address as well as those of each individual owner. If the publication is published by a nonprofit organization, give its name and address.)

Full Name	Complete Mailing Address
Wiley Subscription Services, Inc.	111 River Street, Hoboken, NJ 07030
(see attached list)	

11. Known Bondholders, Mortgagees, and Other Security Holders Owning or Holding 1 Percent or More of Total Amount of Bonds, Mortgages, or Other Securities. If none, check box ► ☑ None

Full Name	Complete Mailing Address
None	

12. Tax Status (For completion by nonprofit organizations authorized to mail at nonprofit rates) (Check one)
The purpose, function, and nonprofit status of this organization and the exempt status for federal income tax purposes:
☐ Has Not Changed During Preceding 12 Months
☐ Has Changed During Preceding 12 Months (Publisher must submit explanation of change with this statement)

PS Form **3526**, October 1999 (See Instructions on Reverse)

---

13. Publication Title	14. Issue Date for Circulation Data Below
New Directions For Institutional Research	Spring 2004

15. Extent and Nature of Circulation		Average No. Copies Each Issue During Preceding 12 Months	No. Copies of Single Issue Published Nearest to Filing Date
a. Total Number of Copies (Net press run)		1913	1930
b. Paid and/or Requested Circulation	(1) Paid/Requested Outside-County Mail Subscriptions Stated on Form 3541. (Include advertiser's proof and exchange copies)	691	711
	(2) Paid In-County Subscriptions Stated on Form 3541 (Include advertiser's proof and exchange copies)	0	0
	(3) Sales Through Dealers and Carriers, Street Vendors, Counter Sales, and Other Non-USPS Paid Distribution	0	0
	(4) Other Classes Mailed Through the USPS	0	0
c. Total Paid and/or Requested Circulation (Sum of 15b. (1), (2),(3),and (4)) ►		691	711
d. Free Distribution by Mail (Samples, complimentary, and other free)	(1) Outside-County as Stated on Form 3541	0	0
	(2) In-County as Stated on Form 3541	0	0
	(3) Other Classes Mailed Through the USPS	0	0
e. Free Distribution Outside the Mail (Carriers or other means)		79	82
f. Total Free Distribution (Sum of 15d. and 15e.) ►		79	82
g. Total Distribution (Sum of 15c. and 15f) ►		770	793
h. Copies not Distributed		1143	1137
i. Total (Sum of 15g. and h.) ►		1913	1930
j. Percent Paid and/or Requested Circulation (15c. divided by 15g. times 100)		89.74%	89.66%

16. Publication of Statement of Ownership

☑ Publication required. Will be printed in the **Fall 2004** issue of this publication. ☐ Publication not required.

17. Signature and Title of Editor, Publisher, Business Manager, or Owner

Susan F. Lewis *(signed)* — Susan E. Lewis, VP & Publisher - Periodicals

Date 10/1/04

I certify that all information furnished on this form is true and complete. I understand that anyone who furnishes false or misleading information on this form or who omits material or information requested on the form may be subject to criminal sanctions (including fines and imprisonment) and/or civil sanctions (including civil penalties).

Instructions to Publishers

1. Complete and file one copy of this form with your postmaster annually on or before October 1. Keep a copy of the completed form for your records.

2. In cases where the stockholder or security holder is a trustee, include in items 10 and 11 the name of the person or corporation for whom the trustee is acting. Also include the names and addresses of individuals who are stockholders who own or hold 1 percent or more of the total amount of bonds, mortgages, or other securities of the publishing corporation. In item 11, if none, check the box. Use blank sheets if more space is required.

3. Be sure to furnish all circulation information called for in item 15. Free circulation must be shown in items 15d, e, and f.

4. Item 15h., Copies not Distributed, must include (1) newsstand copies originally stated on Form 3541, and returned to the publisher, (2) estimated returns from news agents, and (3), copies for office use, leftovers, spoiled, and all other copies not distributed.

5. If the publication had Periodicals authorization as a general or requester publication, this Statement of Ownership, Management, and Circulation must be published; it must be printed in any issue in October or, if the publication is not published during October, the first issue printed after October.

6. In item 16, indicate the date of the issue in which this Statement of Ownership will be published.

7. Item 17 must be signed.

Failure to file or publish a statement of ownership may lead to suspension of Periodicals authorization.

PS Form **3526**, October 1999 (Reverse)

89400126R00088

Made in the USA
Lexington, KY
27 May 2018